Acting Edition

Tumacho

by Ethan Lipton

Additional music compositions and arrangements by Ian M. Riggs

Copyright © 2018 by Ethan Lipton
All Rights Reserved
2022 Revised Edition

TUMACHO is fully protected under the copyright laws of the United States of America, the British Commonwealth, including Canada, and all member countries of the Berne Convention for the Protection of Literary and Artistic Works, the Universal Copyright Convention, and/or the World Trade Organization conforming to the Agreement on Trade Related Aspects of Intellectual Property Rights. All rights, including professional and amateur stage productions, recitation, lecturing, public reading, motion picture, radio broadcasting, television, online/digital production, and the rights of translation into foreign languages are strictly reserved.

ISBN 978-0-573-70707-0

www.concordtheatricals.com
www.concordtheatricals.co.uk

FOR PRODUCTION INQUIRIES

UNITED STATES AND CANADA
info@concordtheatricals.com
1-866-979-0447

UNITED KINGDOM AND EUROPE
licensing@concordtheatricals.co.uk
020-7054-7298

Each title is subject to availability from Concord Theatricals Corp., depending upon country of performance. Please be aware that *TUMACHO* may not be licensed by Concord Theatricals Corp. in your territory. Professional and amateur producers should contact the nearest Concord Theatricals Corp. office or licensing partner to verify availability.

CAUTION: Professional and amateur producers are hereby warned that *TUMACHO* is subject to a licensing fee. The purchase, renting, lending or use of this book does not constitute a license to perform this title(s), which license must be obtained from Concord Theatricals Corp. prior to any performance. Performance of this title(s) without a license is a violation of federal law and may subject the producer and/or presenter of such performances to civil penalties. Both amateurs and professionals considering a production are strongly advised to apply to the appropriate agent before starting rehearsals, advertising, or booking a theatre. A licensing fee must be paid whether the title(s) is presented for charity or gain and whether or not admission is charged. Professional/Stock licensing fees are quoted upon application to Concord Theatricals Corp.

This work is published by Samuel French, an imprint of Concord Theatricals Corp.

No one shall make any changes in this title(s) for the purpose of production. No part of this book may be reproduced, stored in a retrieval system, scanned, uploaded, or transmitted in any form, by any means, now known or yet to be invented, including mechanical, electronic, digital, photocopying, recording, videotaping, or otherwise, without the prior written permission of the publisher. No one shall share this title(s), or any part of this title(s), through any social media or file hosting websites.

For all inquiries regarding motion picture, television, online/digital and other media rights, please contact Concord Theatricals Corp.

MUSIC AND THIRD-PARTY MATERIALS USE NOTE

Licensees are solely responsible for obtaining formal written permission from copyright owners to use copyrighted music and/or other copyrighted third-party materials (e.g., artworks, logos) in the performance of this play and are strongly cautioned to do so. If no such permission is obtained by the licensee, then the licensee must use only original music and materials that the licensee owns and controls. Licensees are solely responsible and liable for clearances of all third-party copyrighted materials, including without limitation music, and shall indemnify the copyright owners of the play(s) and their licensing agent, Concord Theatricals Corp., against any costs, expenses, losses and liabilities arising from the use of such copyrighted third-party materials by licensees. For music, please contact the appropriate music licensing authority in your territory for the rights to any incidental music.

IMPORTANT BILLING AND CREDIT REQUIREMENTS

If you have obtained performance rights to this title, please refer to your licensing agreement for important billing and credit requirements.

Original music by Ethan Lipton is required for performance. Please contact your licensing representative for more information.

TUMACHO was first produced by Clubbed Thumb at the Wild Project as part of the 21st Annual Summerworks in June 2016. The performance was directed by Leigh Silverman, with sets by David Zinn, costumes by Anita Yavich, lights by Jennifer Schriever, props by Raphael Mishler, music direction by Mike Brun, and additional music compositions and arrangements by Ian M. Riggs. The production stage manager was Megan Schwarz Dickert. The cast was as follows:

ALICE WHISTLER	Jennifer Lim
MAYOR EVANS	John Ellison Conlee
DR. ALONZO	Gibson Frazier
PRUDENCE ALDERMAN	Randy Danson
SAM WHISTLER	Bill Buell
CLEMENT GRAHAM JR.	Omary Metwally
WILLIAM "BILL" YARDLEY	Danny Wolohan
CATALINA VUCOVICH-VILLALOBOS	Celia Keenan-Bolger
CHAPPY WING	Jeremy Shamos

TUMACHO was commissioned by Clubbed Thumb, made possible by the New York State Council on the Arts, with the support of Governor Andrew Cuomo and the New York State Legislature.

CHARACTERS

ALICE WHISTLER
MAYOR EVANS
DR. ALONZO
PRUDENCE ALDERMAN
SAM WHISTLER
CLEMENT GRAHAM JR. (AND SR.)
WILLIAM "BILL" YARDLEY
CATALINA VUCOVICH-VILLALOBOS
CHAPPY WING

SETTING

A lousy little town

TIME

The day of the gunfighters

AUTHOR'S NOTE

For the purposes of this play, the word *coyote* rhymes with *zygote*.

Note on Music

Original music by Ethan Lipton is required for performance; this music is available for purchase at samuelfrench.com. Optional music by Ian M. Riggs is available for an additional per-performance fee. Please contact your licensing representative for more information.

SONG LIST

1. "One-Horse Town" .... Cacti & Catalina
2. "Am I Tumacho?" .... Mayor Evans
3. "Chappy's Rap" .... Chappy
4. "We Need a Break" .... Sam, Alice, Catalina, All
5. "No Justice for the Dead" .... Senior & Catalina
6. "I Am Tumacho" .... Prudence
7. "Here I Go" .... Catalina, Mayor Evans, Cacti
8. "Alice's Worries (Am I Tumacho? – Reprise)" .... Alice
9. "Demon Doll" .... Bill
10. "Oh, the Saguaro" .... All

PROLOGUE

[MUSIC NO. 01 "ONE-HORSE TOWN"]
(An unseen **CHOIR** *sings "Ahhs.")*
(The sun climbs over a distant town.)
(On a bluff, a field of **SAGUARO CACTI**, *played by puppets, sing:)*

CACTI.
IN A ONE-HORSE TOWN
WHERE THE HORSE BROKE DOWN
AND THE PONY IS OWNED BY A DEVIL WELL-KNOWN
FOR THE SUFF'RIN' HE SPREADS AROUND

WHEN THE HOPE HAS LEFT
FROM A TOWN BEREFT
AND YOUR LOVED ONES ARE GONE
BUT THEIR MEM'RY LIVES ON
B'SEECHIN' YOU EVEN IN DEATH

YOU MUST HEAR THEIR PLEAS
G'DUP OFF YOUR KNEES
YOU GOT ONE LIFE TO LIVE
BETTER KNOW WHAT TO GIVE
GOTTA DIG IN, HELP BRING LASTING PEACE –

(Enter **CATALINA VUCOVICH-VILLALOBOS**.*)*

CATALINA.
– WITH MURDEROUS, BLOODY REVENGE
MURDEROUS, BLOODY REVENGE
I'LL PLUG UP THE HOLES IN MY HEART
WITH MURDEROUS, BLOODY REVENGE

*(**CATALINA** whips around and fires at the* **CACTI**, *each succulent dying with dramatic flair.)*

(Yet one **CACTUS** *survives, still quaking.* **CATALINA** *approaches.)*

CATALINA. Well, well, well.

*(***CATALINA*** reaches for her gun, and the* **CACTUS** *dies of fright.)*

(The music builds...)

Scene One

(Saloon music.*)

(A border town saloon. **ALICE WHISTLER,** *the barmaid, cleans glasses.)*

*(***CATALINA*** is passed out on the bar, too drunk for words.)*

(A gunshot rings out. **MAYOR EVANS** *enters, howling.)*

MAYOR EVANS. Oh, please God, no. No, no, no!

(He runs to the bathroom. We hear peeing.)

(Offstage.) Thank you, Lord! You are a kind and loving savior, yes you are.

(More peeing.)

Oh, Lord Almighty.

(More peeing.)

And I meant what I said about everything. No more drinking or gossip. No more spicy food or lusting after showgirls. You held up your part of the bargain; now I'm holding up mine.

ALICE. Mayor Evans –

MAYOR EVANS. *(Offstage.)* Alice, dear, with you in a moment!

(More peeing.)

Oh, jeezy creezy. Oh, righteous master of heaven –

---

*Samuel French licenses optional incidental music by Ian M. Riggs. If you choose not to license this optional music, please be aware that a license to produce *Tumacho* does not include a performance license for any third-party or copyrighted music. Licensees should create an original composition or use music in the public domain. For further information, please see the Music and Third-Party Materials Use Note on page iii.

ALICE. I can hear you.

MAYOR EVANS. *(Offstage.)* Yes, but I'm going to the bathroom, dear. If you can just hold on for two shakes, I'll be right there.

> *(More peeing.)*

Dear Lord Almighty, your generosity knows no bounds. Thank you for your kindness –

> *(The sound of one shake.)*

And your mercy.

> *(The sound of a second shake; then a bonus shake.)*
>
> *(**MAYOR EVANS** emerges from the bathroom.)*

Now then. What did you want to tell me, dear? Over a whiskey, if you'd be so tender.

> *(**ALICE** pours the **MAYOR** a shot.)*

ALICE. Your tab is three months overdue.

MAYOR EVANS. Qu'est-ce que c'est? You sure you have the right Mayor Evans?

ALICE. Positive.

MAYOR EVANS. That's troubling. The expense reports must not have been filed. First chance I get, I'll bring it up with the city clerk.

ALICE. And who would that be?

MAYOR EVANS. I'm hiring, if you know any viable candidates. Someone who's good with numbers of course, and they have to be able to think on their feet.

> *(A hail of gunshots is heard, followed by a man's last gasp and a thud.)*

God punish that animal! When is somebody going to put a stop to this violence?

ALICE. I thought that was your job.

MAYOR EVANS. No, Alice, I have a different job. It's called being mayor, and it entails a great many tasks and responsibilities.

ALICE. We had near a thousand people in this town when you took office. Now what do we have, twenty on a good day?

MAYOR EVANS. About half that, and my word are they demanding. *Me, me, me! Where's my clean water? Why can't I walk out of the house without getting shot at? Doody doody doody doo!*

ALICE. Don't they have a right to expect a little safekeeping?

MAYOR EVANS. What do you think a sheriff is for?

ALICE. Lining his pockets with gold.

MAYOR EVANS. Not this one, Alice. Sheriff Ortiz is a man of integrity.

ALICE. He isn't a man at all. The boy is barely eighteen.

MAYOR EVANS. A man, I say, if you measure it in terms of his height and overall appetite. A man who's fought crime on both sides of the border and emerged the victor every time. I'm telling you, Alice, this time I found one who's positively incorruptible.

ALICE. That's what you said about Sheriff Parker.

MAYOR EVANS. Well, Sheriff Parker had a gambling issue.

ALICE. And Sheriff Brown?

MAYOR EVANS. His sister was an invalid, the woman required a staff.

ALICE. How about Sheriff Almgren?

MAYOR EVANS. If I'd known he was Swedish, I'd never have hired him.

ALICE. They all have their excuses, Mayor Evans, and one way or another they all cave in to Bill Yardley. Until they take one in the back or crawl on their bellies out of town. Not that I blame them for leaving.

MAYOR EVANS. Alice.

ALICE. I'd be out of this hole five minutes ago if I wasn't stuck here running this bar for my grandpa.

MAYOR EVANS. How is your grandpa, by the way?

ALICE. You know, senile, depressed, anxious and half-blind.

MAYOR EVANS. Tell him I say hello.

ALICE. I will.

MAYOR EVANS. Alice, Sheriff Ortiz is not like the rest. He crawls for no man, and he's going to bring law and order back to this town *if* – and I know it's a big one, but I think we can do it – *if* we can just give him the time and support that he needs –

CATALINA. *(In a mumbled, drunk sleep.)* Well, well, well...

(**DR. ALONZO** *enters, his coat bloodied.*)

ALICE. Doc Alonzo! Don't tell me *you've* been shot.

DR. ALONZO. I'm afraid it was Sheriff Ortiz.

MAYOR EVANS. Clodhoppers!

DR. ALONZO. He's dead, Mayor Evans. And I need a drink.

ALICE. Poor Sheriff Ortiz.

MAYOR EVANS. Better make mine a double.

ALICE. He was only a child.

DR. ALONZO. And he paid for it. Too many principles, too little fear.

MAYOR EVANS. Did he do any damage before he went down?

DR. ALONZO. Well, he did manage to shoot one of Prudence Alderman's cattle dogs in the leg.

ALICE. Not Pirate I hope.

DR. ALONZO. I didn't catch a name.

ALICE. That dog's the only thing on this earth that makes me smile.

MAYOR EVANS. Aside from your grandpa, of course.

ALICE. Oh, uh-huh, no sure, totally.

DR. ALONZO. Yardley ambushed Ortiz in front of the general store. Yardley said he'd give him one chance to play nice, but Ortiz said he didn't know how and wasn't interested in learning.

MAYOR EVANS. What a dingleberry.

DR. ALONZO. That's when I hit the deck.

ALICE. You were there?

DR. ALONZO. Inside the store, I was buying my beans. Palawski's got a wonderful special on beans right now, I don't know if you saw that, all kinds of beans –

MAYOR EVANS. I noticed the sign –

DR. ALONZO. Kidney beans, lima beans, garbanzo beans –

MAYOR EVANS. I got to get my butt over there –

DR. ALONZO. Better go soon. He's getting out of town.

MAYOR EVANS. Palawski? Says who?

DR. ALONZO. He told me himself.

MAYOR EVANS. Oh, that don't mean nothing. If I had a penny for everyone in this town who claimed they were leaving –

*(**PRUDENCE ALDERMAN** appears at the door.)*

CATALINA. *(Drunken mumble.)* Well, well, well…

PRUDENCE. Mayor Evans, may I have a word?

MAYOR EVANS. Shuttlecock! Don't tell her I'm here.

PRUDENCE. Mayor Evans, I can see you. Mayor Evans?

ALICE. Come on in, Prudence.

PRUDENCE. Thank you, Alice, but you know I can't step foot in this unholy establishment.

ALICE. Just come in. We won't tell nobody.

*(**PRUDENCE** enters.)*

PRUDENCE. Mayor Evans, I assume you've heard –

MAYOR EVANS. About the dog, yes, Prudence, we heard about the dog, and I am – we all are – truly aggrieved over it. But here's the downside to filing a lawsuit against the town –

ALICE. How can you talk about lawsuits when her dog just died?

DR. ALONZO. Oh, I saved the dog.

ALICE. You did?

DR. ALONZO. Yes, and here's how: I fashioned a tourniquet out of my undershirt, which I don't mind telling you I purchased down south from a gentleman with a cart parked in front of a real estate office; I'll never forget, he had a wonderful deal on three-packs, and I told myself at the time, just buy ten of them, you can never have too many undershirts. But alas, I failed to heed my own advice. Doctors! Anyhow, I had to take the dog's leg, Prudence, but if everything proceeds apace, he should make a full recovery.

MAYOR EVANS. You saved the dog, but left the sheriff to die?

DR. ALONZO. There wasn't enough of the sheriff left to save.

ALICE. It wasn't Pirate they shot, I hope.

PRUDENCE. It was.

ALICE. Oh no!

PRUDENCE. I am not here to discuss Pirate, fond of him though I once was and useless though he may be to me now.

DR. ALONZO. But the dog will walk again, Prudence. Or, you know, scootch.

PRUDENCE. I got him to be a work dog, Dr. Alonzo.

DR. ALONZO. Yes but he's still a perfectly nice little –

PRUDENCE. Useless dog.

ALICE. I'll take him.

PRUDENCE. Fine. Mayor Evans, I am here in the wake of recent events to discuss the future of our citizenry, and to hear firsthand how you plan to address it.

MAYOR EVANS. How do I plan to address it? By addressing it. With a plan.

DR. ALONZO. No kidding, Evans, if Yardley keeps going at this clip, there'll be no one left to pick up the pumpkins come autumn.

MAYOR EVANS. I know that, Dr. Alonzo, and I thank you for bringing the impending pumpkin crisis to my attention. Heretofore, the first thing I intend to do as mayor of this town –

ALICE. You're already mayor.

MAYOR EVANS. And I appreciate the vote. Perhaps a parade is in order, to celebrate all we've done right so far –

PRUDENCE. There will be no parade, Mayor Evans.

MAYOR EVANS. Fine then, a summer music festival.

DR. ALONZO. What's the plan, Ignatius?

MAYOR EVANS. May I have a glass of water? Please?

> (**ALICE** *pours* **MAYOR EVANS** *a water. He takes a very long time to drink it.*)

Pretzels, or anything salty?

PRUDENCE. Mayor Evans, I was content if not enthusiastic to conduct my life in this abomination of a town for years past my intended stay, so long as my farm remained profitable, my church remained open, and my affairs remained my own. I was philosophical if not thrilled to learn that the husband I moved here for and whose return from the war I steadfastly awaited had in fact chosen Canada over the warmth of my embrace, and Newfoundland at that. And I was tolerant if not at all pleased when the people of this town began dropping like flies in its barbershops, bingo parlors and smitheries at the hand of Bill Yardley. But if there's one thing I can't stand, Mayor Evans, it's blood in the streets. Now, blood behind closed doors or far out of view? I don't like it but I can ignore it. But blood in the streets? Blood when we walk out of our homes to greet the newborn day? Look at my shoes, Mayor. That's blood. And it isn't dog's blood either, it is the blood of young Sheriff Ortiz. I can learn to live with a lot of things, but I cannot learn to live with blood in our streets.

MAYOR EVANS. What are you trying to say?

ALICE. She's saying you better fix it or else she's hitting the road.

DR. ALONZO. Along with her charitable donations, I surmise.

MAYOR EVANS. Let me ask you something, Prudence. No, back up. Let me ask all of you something. I like you guys, a lot.

ALICE. That's not a question.

MAYOR EVANS. How would you feel if every time you disappointed me, I promised to run off?

DR. ALONZO. Really, Evans?

MAYOR EVANS. *Oh, I don't like the stout tonight, Alice: I guess I'm moving to Fresno!*

PRUDENCE. Good day, Mayor Evans.

MAYOR EVANS. And now you're walking out on me too! See?! This is exactly what I'm talking about.

PRUDENCE. I'm sorry, did you have something to say? Have you ever had something of substance to say? Because I've seen a whole lotta spit fly off of those lips but I don't recall ever hearing much truth.

MAYOR EVANS. I'm trying, Prudence. I am seriously making an effort, like, every day. It makes me sick what's become of this place.

> *(Pointing to **CATALINA**.)*

Take this little vagrant here.

> *(Waking with a start, **CATALINA** pulls a gun on **MAYOR EVANS**.)*

CATALINA. You ain't taking me anywhere!

MAYOR EVANS. *(Lightly pushing her gun away.)* No, Catalina, I was just using you as an example.

CATALINA. Example of what?

MAYOR EVANS. Of someone who once had a promising future.

> *(Pointing to a framed document on the wall.)*

Look at that, first prize in the national fifth-grade essay contest. "Why My Town is the Best."

> *(**CATALINA** passes out on the bar again.)*

PRUDENCE. For the last time, Mayor Evans, we're not speaking of anyone but you.

MAYOR EVANS. Look, most nights I go to bed praying Yardley will shoot me next. And when I wake up to find that he hasn't, I try something new. A different tactic, or the same tactic in a different outfit. Tomorrow I will try something else, and the day after that and the day after that, and I will keep trying, Prudence, until this town is a place we can be proud to call home again or I'm out there behind the church with the rest of the worm meal. Honestly, guys, I don't know what else to do.

PRUDENCE. Well, it isn't much, but it might be the truest thing you've said yet.

MAYOR EVANS. I also think I've been the victim of some real bad timing.

SAM. Alice?

ALICE. Grandpa?

> *(Old* **SAM WHISTLER** *is escorted into the bar by* **CLEMENT GRAHAM JR.,** *a well-dressed stranger.* **SAM** *looks like he's seen a ghost.)*

CATALINA. *(Drunk mumble.)* Well, well, well…

ALICE. What have you done with my grandpa?

CLEMENT. I beg your pardon. I was just riding into town, and I saw this fella wandering around in the corn.

ALICE. He ain't been out of the house in two years. Grandpa, are you alright?

SAM. Alice, did you see it?

ALICE. Now, Grandpa, there wasn't anything you were meant to see.

SAM. The sky, Alice. The clouds are upside down!

ALICE. What?

CLEMENT. There's a storm coming up through the valley. He keeps going on about it.

SAM. Isn't it something?

ALICE. The rain? Are you worried about the rain?

SAM. Not rain, Alice, clouds. They're upside down!

DR. ALONZO. Well, would you look at that.

> *(The others go to look too.)*

MAYOR EVANS. They do seem a bit akimbo, don't they?

ALICE. Is it a twister coming?

DR. ALONZO. Not like any I've seen.

SAM. "When the streets run red with blood, and the clouds go upside down, then the three-legged coyote howls, for Tumacho's back in town."

ALICE & DR. ALONZO. Tumacho?!

MAYOR EVANS. Ha-ha. Very funny. Now, Sam, you're being silly. Doc, maybe you have something to ease old Sam's nerves –

DR. ALONZO. Did you say Tumacho?

SAM. He's back!

MAYOR EVANS. No, he isn't anywhere, actually.

CLEMENT. If you don't mind me asking: Who's Tumacho?

MAYOR EVANS. No one, he's not a real person.

DR. ALONZO. Young man, Tumacho is a demon ghost.

MAYOR EVANS. A piece of folklore. Why are you spreading this garbage?

PRUDENCE. Indeed, Doctor, I would expect more from a man of science.

DR. ALONZO. Science has nothing to do with it, Prudence, and if you appreciated the story of Tumacho, you wouldn't be so quick to judge.

CLEMENT. What story? What ghost?

SAM. Tumacho's the baddest dude this town has ever known.

CLEMENT. Badder than…Big Bill Yardley?

SAM. Ha!

CLEMENT. Tell me more.

MAYOR EVANS. Absolutely not! I forbid it! And that's an executive order!

DR. ALONZO. *(After a moment.)* Hundreds of years ago, a creature so vile he made Yardley look like an altar boy, ran roughshod over these parts. He ate a man's heart – ripped it right out of his chest. And he ravaged the rest of the town until they became his slaves and wasted away to nothing. It's said that by the time he was done, he had just one drop of blood in his body, and that drop was a bilious yellow.

SAM. Oh, friend, you're gonna love Tumacho when you meet him. Unless of course, you turn out to be him.

CLEMENT. Whu-hut?

MAYOR EVANS. Okay, that is enough. For the love of ham, I want everyone to go home, this conversation is over!

CLEMENT. What does he mean, *turn out to be him*?

DR. ALONZO. After Tumacho had his way with our town, he vanished. Some say he went to the mountains. Others say he went to the deserty mountains. Still others say he dug his own grave and buried himself in the town square, along with a bowlful of chicharrónes, which, personally, I have a hard time believing.

ALICE. *(Kinda believes it.)* I don't know...

DR. ALONZO. Whatever became of him, ever since then, according to legend –

MAYOR EVANS. – To legend, my friends, to make-believe, alright?

DR. ALONZO. Tumacho has returned every so many years to inhabit the body of someone who walks the streets of our town, and to do as he pleases until he can satisfy himself no more.

SAM. "When the streets run red with blood, and the clouds go upside down, then the three-legged coyote howls, for Tumacho's back in town."

PRUDENCE. But the streets are full of blood.

DR. ALONZO. And the clouds are definitely upside down.

MAYOR EVANS. Fortunately, we ain't seen a coyote in these parts since Easter.

ALICE. Pirate.

MAYOR EVANS. He's a dog!

PRUDENCE. No. The truth is I bought him from a coyote dealer in Nogales.

MAYOR EVANS. Prudence, why?

PRUDENCE. I thought I could change him.

SAM. It could be you, my friend, that Tumacho comes back to possess. Or it could be me.

ALICE. It could be any one of us.

CLEMENT. Can you control it? If Tumacho takes over, can you make him do what you want?

[MUSIC NO. 02 "AM I TUMACHO?"]

(The question tempts them all...)

(The guitar strums.)

MAYOR EVANS.
AM I TUMACHO? COULD I BE THE ONE?
THE ANGEL WITH A KNIFE IN HIS HEART AND LUST IN HIS GUN
AM I TUMACHO? COULD HE BE ME?
AND COULD I IMPOSE MY OWN WILL? COULD I DEBILITATE BILL?

ALL.
AM I TUMACHO? COULD I BE THE ONE?
THE DUDE WITH A RAZOR FOR EYES AND A WHIP FOR A TONGUE
AM I TUMACHO? COULD HE BE ME?
AND COULD I GET SOME FROM EVERY LAST ONE THAT I SEE?
OH, I'M SURE IT'D BE FUN, COULD I BE THE ONE...?
AM I TUMACHO...?

BILL. Afternoon, everybody.

*(**BILL YARDLEY** enters the bar.)*

ALL BUT CLEMENT. *(Cowed.)* Bill.

BILL. Who do we have here?

CLEMENT. They call me Clement Graham Junior.

BILL. Son of quick-draw Clement Graham?

CLEMENT. That's right.

BILL. How is that, having a famous gunfighter for a father?

*(All but **BILL**, **CLEMENT**, and **CATALINA** – who suddenly sits upright in her stool – step toward the door and freeze [as in a game of "red light, green light"].)*

CLEMENT. It has its advantages.

BILL. I'll bet.

CLEMENT. I consider myself quite fortunate to have gotten his good looks and eternally youthful bearing. Not to mention his talent.

BILL. That your mustang out there? With the pelican horn and Cheyenne roll?

CLEMENT. Might be.

BILL. Did you get it for your birthday? Let me guess, for your sixteenth birthday?

CLEMENT. Possibly.

BILL. That's gotta be one of the prettiest rigs I've seen. I could use a horse and saddle like that.

CLEMENT. Well, I'm not selling.

BILL. Oh, I'm not buying.

*(The **OTHERS** exit the bar –)*

MAYOR EVANS. He's a dead man –

DR. ALONZO. This is gonna be ugly –

*(– Then quickly reappear outside, above and below a window, listening in. **CATALINA** slowly reaches for her gun.)*

BILL. I wonder though, does everyone want to go through life on a pony that screams, "Look at me!"?

CLEMENT. Yes.

BILL. See, if you were my son, instead of trying to buy your affection with the world's prettiest horse and saddle, what I'd do is ask what you want for your birthday. To which you might reply, "Well Daddy, what I'd really like is to go camping with you." And then, years later, when the time was right, you could choose your own mode of transportation, though you might not long to travel far, for all you'd really want is to be around me, the one person who knows and understands you. Or I could do what your daddy did: buy you a fancy rig, never have a real conversation, and wake up one day to find you've ridden off without saying goodbye.

CLEMENT. How would you know if I said goodbye to my daddy or didn't?

BILL. If you'd told him you were coming here, son, he'd never have let you go.

CLEMENT. Unless he sent me on his behalf.

BILL. Are you saying that he did?

CLEMENT. I am not.

BILL. So you're saying that he didn't.

CLEMENT. Or am I?

BILL. I don't have any idea what you're saying.

CLEMENT. Here's one thing I've learned. Unless you're my daddy, who can still shoot a man while bedding a maiden three years into retirement, you have to be careful when talking about guns. See, because, if you walk into a town boasting, "Oh, I shot this one guy here, and then I also shot this other guy in Texas," then everyone you meet wants to see you back it up, and it's "draw, draw, draw" every time you buy bread. On the other hand, if you ride into town all, "Cheerio, nuttin' but good intentions here, suh," then everyone's like, "Well, this chump thinks he's better'n me," and it's "draw, draw, draw" from a whole other direction. So, I prefer not to say anything about my taste for violence, and that way everyone's like, "What's this guy's deal? I can't get a read on him. Is he badder than I am? And do I really want to find out?"

BILL. Son, do you know who I am?

CLEMENT. Big Bill Yardley.

BILL. That's right.

CLEMENT. You're what my daddy would call a ne'er-do-well.

BILL. I have a lot of respect for your daddy. There was a time when we exchanged letters, trying to arrange for a duel; we couldn't make the dates work. But what I would tell him, if he was here, is that he is wrong in his opinion of me. For I am many things but a ne'er-do-well isn't one of them. As anyone in our town will tell you, I *do* do well – every time.

CLEMENT. I'm sorry?

BILL. I said I *do* do well: every time.

CLEMENT. Again, this ear, I have a bit of a cold.

BILL. I said I do-do well!

> *(Outside, the **OTHERS** snicker. And **BILL** gives them a hard look.)*

And it's not to luck or bad intentions that I owe my success, but to consistency. See, every day when I wake up, I have a cup of coffee, and then I do-do well: by taking care of business; which is to say, by making sure I'm richer than I was the day before.

The best thing about my little routine is that I don't have to think about it. When I see something I want – a pretty horse, a sheriff's ring –

> *(**BILL** pulls out a ring from his pocket – it's still attached to a finger.)*

– I just take it.

> *(**BILL** removes the ring, then tosses the finger. **CLEMENT** tries to catch it but misses.)*

I don't have to waste time worrying about right and wrong, and I don't have to screw around calling people names.

> *(**BILL** has approached **CLEMENT** and now stands nose-to-nose with him.)*

PRUDENCE. I won't watch.

> *(**PRUDENCE** exits.)*

CLEMENT. *(Now sweating but not flinching.)* Mr. Yardley, you are wise to feel intimidated.

BILL. Mr. Graham, you are about to die confused.

CLEMENT. Are you sure about that?

BILL. Yup.

CLEMENT. *(Swallows hard.)* Well then, perhaps this is a good time to tell you something that has been unknown to you in all the moments prior to the one that is now.

For while it is true that back home I was known to many as Clement Graham Junior, you might know me better as: Tumacho.

OTHERS. *(Popping up in the window.)* Tumacho?!

> *(CATALINA spins around on her stool and points a gun at BILL's head.)*

CLEMENT. Lo these many years I looked down upon this valley, separated from my true self by a false identity, held captive in a hacienda of privilege and misunderstanding until the curse of this town called out like a siren to set me free.

CATALINA. Well, well, well.

CATALINA.	**CLEMENT.**
Ever since I was twelve years old I've been getting ready to make you pay for what you did.	And now I've come home, to my real home, to accept my destiny as the baddest man in town –

BILL. I can't understand either one of you.

CLEMENT. I'm Tumacho.

CATALINA. *(To CLEMENT.)* And I'm Catalina Vucovich-Villalobos. And I can't let you near this man, for it is my life's mission to destroy him.

BILL. May I inquire –

CLEMENT. I have come down from the mountains –

BILL. *(To CLEMENT.)* Excuse me.

(To CATALINA.) Catalina, what is the nature of your grievance?

CATALINA. I'm pretty sure you know.

BILL. But I don't.

CATALINA. Hannah Vucovich. Emilio Villalobos?

BILL. These were people?

CATALINA. They were my parents.

CLEMENT. I am ready to rain terror –

CATALINA. The day you got here, they started making plans to leave. One morning they hid me under a blanket, along with everything we had, and headed for the county line, but you caught up to our coach, didn't you? Said we couldn't leave until we paid a fee. My mama gave you her purse, and you emptied your chamber into them both. Sound familiar now, Bill?

BILL. I mean, vaguely.

CATALINA. You murdered my parents.

BILL. I believe you.

CATALINA. You don't remember?

(BILL shrugs.)

My daddy never thought I had what it took –

(CATALINA points her gun at BILL again.)

CATALINA. I waited for someone to bring you to justice. The mayor and all his stooge sheriffs –

MAYOR EVANS. Hey –

CATALINA. – The meetings they had, the debates, everyone going on, and nobody doing a thing. One time, they spent a whole meeting just setting up the next meeting. That's when I knew that killing you would have to be my destiny. That's why I've been out on that bluff, practicing every day, until my hand hurt so bad, I couldn't even open it.

CLEMENT. I am a demon!

CATALINA. *(To CLEMENT.)* Well you can do what you want with the rest, demon, but this one's mine.

BILL. What took you so long, Catalina? All these years, you knew where to find me.

CATALINA. I guess I needed something to look forward to.

(CATALINA cocks her gun – just as CHAPPY WING enters, arms open wide.)

CHAPPY. Catalina, you're awake!

CATALINA. Chappy, stay back.

CHAPPY. Just a hug?

CATALINA. I'm not playing games, Chappy, please don't touch me!

CHAPPY. Brush up against my leg?

> (**CHAPPY** *keeps coming, and* **CATALINA** *fires a warning shot. The shot ricochets and* **CHAPPY** *leaps to the floor for cover.*)

CLEMENT. *(Wincing.)* Oh.

CHAPPY. What'd you do that for?!

CATALINA. I told you I wasn't messing around.

> *(Collecting herself.)*

Bill, you got anything left to say?

BILL. I think you shot Tumacho.

CHAPPY. Tumacho?!

> (**CLEMENT**, *now holding a hand to the side of his bleeding neck, waves hello.*)

CATALINA. You bleed?

CLEMENT. Uh…

CHAPPY. But that's red.

CLEMENT. Well, I don't think it's much to worry about. Though a napkin might be a good idea.

CATALINA. It ain't possible.

CLEMENT. Or a towel would be fine. Kerchief?

CHAPPY. Tumacho don't have but one drop of blood in all his body, and that drop is a bilious yeller.

CLEMENT. So then?

> *(A woozy* **CLEMENT** *wobbles, and* **CATALINA** *rushes to catch him.* **BILL** *swoops in to disarm* **CATALINA**, *taking her captive.*)

BILL. You, son, are no Tumacho.

CATALINA. But you kept saying –

CLEMENT. Well, I felt like Tumacho, in my heart. Really I just wanted to show my daddy…that I'm awesome.

> (**CLEMENT** *expires. A coyote howls.*)

*(**BILL** drags **CATALINA** to the bar and ties her to it.)*

BILL. Chappy, wannabes don't concern me, but a genuine demon will not be tolerated. If Tumacho is back, we better get him before he gets us. You stay here and guard Catalina.

CHAPPY. Okay.

*(**BILL** cuts **CHAPPY**'s hand, drawing blood.)*

Ayyy...

BILL. I'll check the others, make sure they all bleed pure red. Then we will know if the demon is returned.

*(**BILL** goes to **CATALINA**, draws blood from her hand.)*

Ah, yes. Emilio and Hannah. I remember now. They held hands.

Scene Two

[MUSIC NO. 03 "CHAPPY'S RAP"]

*(In the saloon, **CHAPPY** guards **CATALINA**, who's still tied to the bar. **SAM**'s here too, also tied up. All three wear makeshift bandages on one hand.)*

CHAPPY. *(A spoken-word type thing, accompanied by the banjo.)* Catalina, you know that I don't blame you
for discharging your weapon in my direction.
You didn't mean to hurt no one
except for Bill, who killed your parents.
You made a very simple request, you said:
"Chappy, please don't touch me"
and I took that to mean:
"Please don't touch me very much."

Catalina, I've been misunderstanding
all the messages of this world
since I was but a grassy little hopper
and you were just a pretty little girl.
Sometimes life says, "Chappy, wait:
That ain't chocolate pudding!"
And like a fool I think it's saying:
"So why don't you taste it and find out what it really is."

When the good Lord gave out common sense,
I was fishing with my cousin John.
And when John slipped on a rock and fell into the river,
I was busy making sandwiches.
So I didn't see John drift away or hear him call my name,
if in fact he did,
but that's the day I discovered
my passion for food preparation.

See, 'cause sometimes, Catalina,

a funny thing happens when you get life wrong.
You find that out of ignorance
comes a blessing wrapped in song.
Such as me bugging you to the point where you had to
fire a warning shot and us having this time together,
just a couple of dear old friends,
still a'wonderin' whether –

But all I have to say on that subject
is let the bygones play through.
Why, as soon as I saw you tied up and helpless,
Catalina, I knew:
That I would rather get naked with the devil
than to stay sore at you.
For if this heart doesn't beat for your love
then those eyes are not blue.

CATALINA. Chappy?

CHAPPY. I can't set you free, Catalina.

CATALINA. I know.

CHAPPY. I just can't. If it weren't for Bill, I don't know where I'd be now. Still trying to start my own hostage negotiation company, I guess.

CATALINA. I never knew you had a hostage negotiation company.

CHAPPY. Well, Bill talked me out of it.

CATALINA. Chappy, can I see that gun for a minute?

CHAPPY. This gun?

CATALINA. You can have it right back.

CHAPPY. No, I don't think so.

CATALINA. Chappy, please –

CHAPPY. Listen, Catalina, I know you got a beef with Bill –

CATALINA. He ain't the one I'm aiming for now.

CHAPPY. What?! Is it...me?

CATALINA. No.

CHAPPY. Is it Sam?

CATALINA. No.

CHAPPY. Mayor Evans?

CATALINA. No.

CHAPPY. Doc Alonzo?

CATALINA. No.

CHAPPY. Alice?

CATALINA. No.

CHAPPY. Is it Prudence?

CATALINA. Chappy, I killed an innocent man. All I'm asking for is the chance to do the honorable thing.

(Waits for him to get it, then:)

It's me, Chappy. I'm gonna shoot myself.

CHAPPY. But you didn't kill that man on purpose.

CATALINA. I dedicated my life to murder, didn't I? Well murder is what I got. Now, be a pal, won't ya?

CHAPPY. How about a piece of that candied summer squash you love so much –

CATALINA. Give me the gun.

CHAPPY. Catalina, this town needs you.

CATALINA. This town? This town is as hopeless as I am, and it and me both are gonna rot in hell.

CHAPPY. You don't really believe that.

CATALINA. Chappy, what do you think, in your wildest dreams, is the best that could ever become of us?

CHAPPY. I mean, I think we could stay in touch, until one day we figure there's just no use fighting it anymore and ride off into the sunset together.

CATALINA. I was asking about the town.

CHAPPY. Oh, right, ha! And I'm like "rhjuh-rhjuh-rhjuh-rhjuh!" Well geez, Catalina, I don't know. All I know is, you got to believe in something, or else there ain't no point in living.

CATALINA. I couldn't have said it better myself.

*(**CATALINA** holds her hand out, asking for the gun.)*

CHAPPY. What if Tumacho comes back and he gets rid of Bill?

CATALINA. Then you've just replaced one demon with another.

CHAPPY. What if we train Tumacho to be our friend and give him assignments, like "make us a railroad."

CATALINA. I don't imagine he'd take well to instruction.

CHAPPY. Darn it Catalina, there has to be something we can hope for!

CATALINA. I don't know what. Not unless you want to bank on the ineffable.

CHAPPY. What's that?

CATALINA. It's something you can't even describe.

CHAPPY. You could describe it to me.

CATALINA. No, I can't.

CHAPPY. Why not?

CATALINA. There just ain't words for it, Chappy.

CHAPPY. Well, what's the word you used a second ago?

CATALINA. Ineffable.

CHAPPY. So what's that mean?

CATALINA. I'm telling you, it's something you can't articulate.

CHAPPY. But I could try to, if you gave me the definition!

CATALINA. I can't tell you what it is because I don't know!

[MUSIC NO. 04 "WE NEED A BREAK"]

SAM.
IT'S A TWIST OF FATE, IT'S A SUDDEN TURN
IT'S A HELPING HAND WE MIGHT NEVER DISCERN
IT'S A SAVING GRACE FROM A SACRED PLACE
OH FOR HEAVEN'S SAKE, IT'S A LUCKY BREAK

*(From around town, all but **BILL** drift into the bar on a chain gang. Each one has been cut and bandaged. They hum.)*

ALL.
> WE NEED A BREAK
> GIVE US A BREAK
> THIS TAKES THE CAKE –

ALICE.
> THIS LIFE OF ENDLESS SUFFERING

ALL.
> WE NEED A BREAK

SAM. It ain't easy living in a time that's hopeless, in a place full of troubles that won't never be fixed. But sometimes the hardest thing to do is just hang in there, keep your head down, and assume that a miracle will save the day...

ALL.
> WE NEED A BREAK

SAM. ...I know that's what I'm doing!

ALL.
> GIVE US A BREAK
> REAL OR FAKE, BY CHANCE OR MISTAKE
> WE NEED A BREAK

MEN.
> A MOTHER-LOVING BREAK!

CATALINA.
> IT'S A PUFF OF SMOKE IN THE DEAD OF NIGHT
> IT'S A COLD WIND BLOWING

ALL.
> IT'S A WILD HAIR GROWING

CATALINA.
> IT'S A WRONG SO WRONG THAT IT MAKES THINGS RIGHT
> IT'S AN ACT OF MERCY THAT YOU CAN'T EXPLAIN

(The **OTHERS** *"ooh" as:)*

Chappy, I know what I have to do!

CHAPPY. You're gonna dress up like a badger and move into my cellar?

CATALINA. No, I'm gonna find that Clement Graham's father and confess to what I've done.

CHAPPY. What? Why?

CATALINA. So he can be the one who kills me.

CHAPPY. But –

CATALINA. I know what it feels like to have someone you love stolen from you. If I give that man the justice he deserves, then maybe he can move on with his life, instead of throwing it away like I did mine.

CHAPPY. But we could probably use your help around here –

CATALINA. Goodbye, old friend. Fare thee well.

> (**CATALINA** *chews through the ropes that bind her and exits.*)

ALL.
>WE NEED A BREAK
>GIVE US A BREAK
>THROW US A BONE, WE DON'T MEAN TO MOAN
>WE JUST WANT OUR OLD HOME
>AND A MOTHER, MOTHER, MOTHER-LOVING –

BILL. *(Entering.)* Good news, people. I checked out every last one of you – even gave myself a poke – and I drew red blood every time. You know what that means, don't you?

DR. ALONZO. No Tumacho?

BILL. That's right. The demon will not be returning at this time.

SAM. God damn it.

BILL. So everyone can go back to the life they were living.

> (*Sighs of disappointment.* **BILL** *unties everyone and they file out.*)

Let's see some smiles, huh? Victory for the status quo.

> (*Sizing up* **PRUDENCE**.)

Prudence? Prudence, I'm talking to you.

PRUDENCE. *(Lingering behind, her voice now grizzled and two octaves lower than before.)* Yes, I am very glad that no one here is a demon.

BILL. I hope I didn't hurt you too bad, when I tackled you out behind the dairy.

PRUDENCE. No.

BILL. I noticed you seemed to go down kinda hard.

PRUDENCE. Well, you were just so strong.

BILL. Listen, I don't know quite how to say this but it looks like you've got some kind of a swelling.

PRUDENCE. Where?

BILL. There, around the midsection.

PRUDENCE. I don't see it.

BILL. Prudence, I think you've got an abscess or, I don't know what it is, but it sure does look lumpy.

> (**PRUDENCE** *slaps* **BILL.** *He rips open her blouse, revealing a calfskin bag tied to her corset.*)

What's that?

PRUDENCE. Haven't you ever seen a corset?

BILL. On top of the corset! You got a bag of something, right there.

PRUDENCE. What, you mean this bag of blood?

BILL. Bag of blood? Prudence, why would you be carrying around a bag of blood?

> (*Scary music, like from an old-time movie.**)
>
> (**PRUDENCE** *takes* **BILL** *in her arms and ravages him.* **BILL** *fights back at first but quickly succumbs to her will. Lightning flashes and thunder roars.*)

---

*Samuel French licenses optional incidental music by Ian M. Riggs. If you choose not to license this optional music, please be aware that a license to produce *Tumacho* does not include a performance license for any third-party or copyrighted music. Licensees should create an original composition or use music in the public domain. For further information, please see the Music and Third-Party Materials Use Note on page iii.

Scene Three

(Tinkly depressive piano music.*)

(The saloon. It's raining outside. Spirits are low. **ALICE** *preps a bowl of food.)*

ALICE. Here, boy.

  *(***ALICE*** sets the bowl down behind the bar. We hear a dog's chirpy bark.)*

That's a good Pirate.

PIRATE. *(Offstage.)* Chirp.

ALICE. You like that food? Is that some tasty food I made for you?

PIRATE. *(Offstage.)* Chirp-chirp.

ALICE. And tell me honest, do you prefer chicken or would you rather have beef?

PIRATE. *(Offstage.)* Chirrr…chirp-chirp chirp-chirp, chirp chirp chirp-chirp?

ALICE. Mm-hm? Anything mixed in with that?

PIRATE. *(Offstage.)* Chirp chirp chirp?

ALICE. Chicken with cheese and beans it is.

PIRATE. *(Offstage, eats; then, saying her name.)* Chirp-chirp?

ALICE. Yes?

PIRATE. *(Offstage.)* Chirp chirp chirp chirp chirp chirp-chirp? Chirp chirp chirp chirp chirp chirp Tumacho?

ALICE. I don't know, Pirate. But I wish I did.

  (Enter **MAYOR EVANS.***)*

---

*Samuel French licenses optional incidental music by Ian M. Riggs. If you choose not to license this optional music, please be aware that a license to produce *Tumacho* does not include a performance license for any third-party or copyrighted music. Licensees should create an original composition or use music in the public domain. For further information, please see the Music and Third-Party Materials Use Note on page iii.

MAYOR EVANS. Alice, you were right. I'm not the man to lead this town, and it was foolish of me to try. Now, upon seeing this fact, way too late – always too late, for Christ's sake, every epiphany I ever have comes ten to fifteen years after it should; nevertheless – I've turned in my resignation, and it's time for me to move on.

ALICE. You're just gonna pick up and run, huh?

MAYOR EVANS. That is correct.

ALICE. Leave the rest of us behind?

MAYOR EVANS. Only the others. Alice, I want you to come with.

ALICE. Excuse me?

MAYOR EVANS. Come with me, Alice. Be my companion.

ALICE. Why?

MAYOR EVANS. Why?

ALICE. Why would I do that?

MAYOR EVANS. Because this town is becrapped. Because Yardley's getting meaner by the minute, Tumacho ain't coming and because I want you to. Alice, you're the most special woman I've ever known.

ALICE. Really.

MAYOR EVANS. Yes. And the funniest and the funnest *and* the smartest *and* the most beautiful.

ALICE. I'm not *that* fun.

MAYOR EVANS. You have skills, Alice. You know geography and you speak Spanish, and you sing like a bird in Spanish. I know I'm not much to look at. And yes, I'm twenty years older, and a lifetime of gum disease – I don't know if you can see the dark spots back here –

ALICE. Uh-huh?

MAYOR EVANS. – Has left me with this musty, sort of mothbally taste I can never quite shake.

ALICE. Uh-huh?

MAYOR EVANS. I don't know how to cook and I can't build a house. But I like to drink and talk until the wee hours of the morn, and I could keep you company while you build us a home.

ALICE. Tempting as that sounds, Mayor Evans, it's not a move I can see myself making at this time. I could never abandon my grandpa.

MAYOR EVANS. And you think he'd notice?

ALICE. Of course he would.

MAYOR EVANS. Because sometimes I'll be talking to him, and he'll just start drooling, and I wonder –

ALICE. I think he would notice if I never came home.

MAYOR EVANS. What if we brought him with us?

ALICE. Well, then there's Pirate to worry about.

MAYOR EVANS. Alice, you're talking about a compromised three-legged coyote –

ALICE. *(Genuinely wanting to go.)* Damn you, Evans!

(Considers.)

Maybe I have wondered what it would be like to live in a better circumstance. To move away to a big city where the people wear sweaters and live in tiny compartments, like ants all stacked on top of each other. But that's just the stuff of dreams, okay? If life was supposed to be fulfilling, I think it would've happened by now. But you go. Go on, explore the world, see all the latest crazes, but just remember: There are three guns for every lunatic out there, and there's at least fifty thousand lunatics, so that's about twelve million lunatics with guns.

MAYOR EVANS. *(Trying to do the math.)* Alice, I'm not sure that adds up quite right –

ALICE. Just go. If Bill finds out you're planning to leave, you'll never get out of here alive.

*(**DR. ALONZO** enters, a mellower, more vacant, zombie-like version of himself, his head bobbling ever so slightly.)*

DR. ALONZO. A lager, please.

MAYOR EVANS. Doc, I'm getting out of town.

DR. ALONZO. Best of luck to you then.

MAYOR EVANS. I just don't see a better alternative.

DR. ALONZO. Safe travels.

MAYOR EVANS. Of course, there won't be a presiding mayor now, so you might want to appoint one on an interim basis.

DR. ALONZO. Will do.

MAYOR EVANS. You feeling okay, Doc?

DR. ALONZO. Fine. You?

MAYOR EVANS. Yeah, I mean I'm scared, more than a little melancholy. This is the only place I've ever lived.

DR. ALONZO. Now there'll be another.

>   (**BILL**, **SAM**, *and* **CHAPPY** *enter, zombie-like, all three spacier than before, heads bobbling ever so slightly.*)

BILL, CHAPPY & SAM. A lager please.

MAYOR EVANS. Oh my, Chappy, Sam...Bill.

BILL. Alice, a round of drinks, please. And one for you, and maybe an extra just in case.

>   (**ALICE** *pours them all drinks.*)

MAYOR EVANS. Well, guess I'll just head back to the office, catch up on my compliance reports.

>   (**PRUDENCE** *enters.*)

PRUDENCE. *(Voice still low and distorted.)* A lager, please.

MAYOR EVANS. Prudence, you drink?

PRUDENCE. On special occasions.

BILL. *(Raising his glass.)* To Prudence.

ALL. To Prudence!

>   *(They drink.)*

PRUDENCE. Thank you so much. You must be quite relieved, Mayor Evans, to know that the demon is not among us.

MAYOR EVANS. Absolutely, full of relief.

PIRATE. *(Offstage.)* Chirp-chirp!
PRUDENCE. Is that Pirate?
ALICE. Uh-huh.

> *(PRUDENCE joins ALICE behind the bar.)*

Did you want to say hi?
PRUDENCE. May I? Have you ever seen his birthmark?
ALICE. No.
PRUDENCE. Here, I'll show you.

> *(PRUDENCE ducks down below the bar and we hear her ravaging PIRATE.)*

ALICE. Oh, I don't know if he likes that.
PRUDENCE. Look closer.

> *(PRUDENCE yanks ALICE below the bar and ravages her for a long time.)*

MAYOR EVANS. *(Truly scared.)* Alice? Uh, Alice?

> *(ALICE and PRUDENCE pop up from behind the bar, ALICE now a spacier version of herself, head bobbling slightly.)*

ALICE. Anyone need a lager?
CHAPPY, SAM & DR. ALONZO. A lager, please.
BILL. *(His head now pierced with pain.)* Oh, my head.
SAM. *(Head in pain.)* Ow!
MAYOR EVANS. Alice. Could I have a word with you? In private?
PRUDENCE. Do you have something to hide, Mayor Evans?
MAYOR EVANS. Certainly not.
PRUDENCE. Then why don't you share it with everyone?
CHAPPY. *(Grabbing his head.)* Ow!
MAYOR EVANS. It's you, isn't it?
PRUDENCE. Who?
MAYOR EVANS. Tumacho.
PRUDENCE. Hello.
MAYOR EVANS. So, how's this gonna work?

PRUDENCE. Well, first I'm gonna suck out the poison.

MAYOR EVANS. Poison?

PRUDENCE. In your blood.

MAYOR EVANS. Shoot. You're gonna suck out all my blood?

PRUDENCE. Suck out the blood to get the poison, suck out the poison to get the blood.

MAYOR EVANS. Do you put the blood back in?

PRUDENCE. Blood comes back on its own, so I can suck out the poison again. I also like candy and yak –

MAYOR EVANS. It's gonna hurt, isn't it?

PRUDENCE. Only for a minute. Then you get kinda dizzy and everything tingles. Then you get thirsty, and then the headache begins.

DR. ALONZO. *(Head hurting.)* Oh.

PRUDENCE. – And the achiness, followed by vomiting and darkness.

MAYOR EVANS. Darkness?

PRUDENCE. It's best not to discuss.

*(Offstage, **PIRATE** begins to moan.)*

ALICE. *(In pain.)* My head –

PRUDENCE. But before you know it, you'll be feeling like your old self, and that's when I'll know it's time to start all over again.

*(**PRUDENCE** takes the **MAYOR** in her arms.)*

(She roars, about to ravage him –)

MAYOR EVANS. Oh, mercy!

(– But the demon gags, oddly repulsed.)

PRUDENCE. Yeee...

*(**PRUDENCE** rears back again –)*

MAYOR EVANS. *(Anticipating pain, not actually feeling it.)* Ouch-ouch-ouch-ouch-ouch-ouch-ouch-ouch-ouch–

(– But the demon gags again.)

PRUDENCE. Gyah...

*(**PRUDENCE** rears back one last time, gags, then gives up and drops **MAYOR EVANS** to the ground.)*

Nope.

Scene Four

(Traveling music.*)

(A tiny puppet Catalina rides a tiny horse up a tiny mountain. The moon sets and the sun rises, then the sun sets and the moon rises. The sun rises again and Catalina rides.)

*(Finally, a bedraggled, full-sized **CATALINA** crawls onstage, collapsing before a great hacienda at the feet of **CLEMENT GRAHAM SR.**, a man who is the spitting image of his son [and played by the same actor]. **CATALINA** is so tired and thirsty, her tongue so swollen, she can barely speak.)*

SENIOR. Can I help you?

CATALINA. Ho so. Oh, you luh juh lyum.

SENIOR. Would you like to stand up?

CATALINA. Nah yeh. Cashm breff.

SENIOR. I hope you didn't walk here. Where's your horse?

CATALINA. He got tire. Tie em up bih big cottonwood tree. I din theek it be tho far.

SENIOR. Yeah, there's about twenty miles of trail after that.

CATALINA. Lon way.

SENIOR. Can I bring you some water?

CATALINA. No-no.

SENIOR. Are you sure?

CATALINA. Yeah-yeah. Haddum yedderay.

SENIOR. Well, I think you're allowed to have some again today. Gee, your tongue got all swole up, didn't it?

---

*Samuel French licenses optional incidental music by Ian M. Riggs. If you choose not to license this optional music, please be aware that a license to produce *Tumacho* does not include a performance license for any third-party or copyrighted music. Licensees should create an original composition or use music in the public domain. For further information, please see the Music and Third-Party Materials Use Note on page iii.

CATALINA. You Cleb Gra, ry?

SENIOR. I am. And you are?

CATALINA. Ca-alina... Vuvavoo... Ca-alina... Voovoojoojoo... Ca...

SENIOR. That's okay, Catalina, yes, I am Clement Graham. Now what can I do for you?

CATALINA. Iguh tell you some... Some bad.

SENIOR. Well come on in, you can tell me inside.

CATALINA. No go side.

(Looks around the home, whistles admiringly.)

Hey, ni play.

SENIOR. Thank you. I just redid the pavilion. Got some help coming over on Friday, we're gonna put a tempera wash on all those arches.

CATALINA. Your thun die.

SENIOR. How's that?

CATALINA. Your thun, Clebba. Tho thar.

SENIOR. Clem Junior? Dead?

CATALINA. I thought-mm. We wuh idduh thand-off. Nah me Cleb, me Yarley.

SENIOR. Big Bill Yardley?

CATALINA. Clebba dere. I fie: warning thought, *pishew*. Ry neck.

SENIOR. You hit Clem in the neck? With a, what, with a ricochet?

CATALINA. Rithay. Tho thar.

SENIOR. Son of a gun. My little boy. Seems like just yesterday he was running up these hills, bossing around the buffalo.

(Considers.)

Well, if he had to go early, I'm glad he got to do it around interesting people.

CATALINA. He wah to impret you.

SENIOR. Yeah, well, Bill Yardley's no slouch. Used to be one of the finest leather-workers in the territory, until ol' Ginger up and left him. Thank you, Miss Voovoo Joojoo, for coming all this way to give me the news about my son. Now please, let me bring you inside. We'll get you some food and water and put some aloe on those blisters.

CATALINA. Yooga kih me, ry?

SENIOR. Kill you?

CATALINA. Yeah.

SENIOR. No, ma'am.

CATALINA. Ih tokay. You cuh do ih.

SENIOR. Darling, if there's one thing I learned in all my years of gunfighting, it's that people die, even ones you care for. And there ain't nothing you can do to bring them back.

CATALINA. Tho...ah you thay, you buh-dib me?

SENIOR. I buh-what what?

CATALINA. You buh-dib me?

SENIOR. Oh, forgive. I mean, well... I understand you didn't mean to do it, and I don't harbor anything against you. But I don't believe forgiveness is mine to offer.

CATALINA. You doh buh-dib me?

SENIOR. That's what I'm getting at, it ain't within my power. If you want forgiveness, I'm afraid you'll have to give it to yourself.

CATALINA. Buh I kah gibbit to mytel.

SENIOR. Why not?

CATALINA. I hay Yarley my ho lie. He kih ma parenh. I plah reven, many yih, buh i doh good, doot Clem i'tead. Cuh iba ba burdun.

SENIOR. A bad person?

CATALINA. Yeah, eeble ba. And I'm naw guh leeb dih play uddil you doot me oh you buhdib me.

[MUSIC NO. 05 "NO JUSTICE FOR THE DEAD"]

SENIOR.
>RUB YOUR TUMMY, PAT YOUR HEAD
>THERE CAN BE NO JUSTICE FOR THE DEAD
>IT'S A SHADY LITTLE SECRET BUT IT MUST BE SAID
>THERE CAN BE NO JUSTICE FOR THE DEAD

CATALINA. Whuh you doin?

SENIOR.
>TOUCH YOUR FINGERS TO YOUR TOES
>HOW DO WE KEEP ON GOING?
>HEAVEN KNOWS
>THERE'S NO HIDING FROM THE FEELING WHEN THE COLD WIND BLOWS
>THERE CAN BE NO JUSTICE FOR THE DEAD

Join me for the rest?

CATALINA. I doh know it.

SENIOR. Are you sure?

SENIOR & CATALINA.
>THERE ARE LONG AND RESTLESS NIGHTS
>WHEN WE'RE LOOKING FOR ANOTHER FIGHT
>AND WE'RE FISHING FOR A REASON
>TO BELIEVE IT'S ALL BEEN WORTH IT INSTEAD
>BUT HERE'S A CRAZY ALLEGATION, 'CAUSE IT MUST BE SAID
>THERE CAN BE NO JUSTICE FOR THE DEAD

CATALINA. Dih wunt what I at for.

SENIOR. I know.
>CLOSE YOUR EYES NOW, TAKE MY HAND

SENIOR & CATALINA.
>EVEN KNUCKLEHEADS LIKE US CAN UNDERSTAND

CATALINA. *[It's a wicked supposition for a heartsick land]*
>IT A WICKA DUPPA-DITTUH FUH'UH HAHDDICK LAN

SENIOR & CATALINA.
>THERE CAN BE NO JUSTICE FOR THE DEAD

SENIOR.
> IT MAY HANG US UP AND BUST US

CATALINA.
> NO ONE'LL EBER TRUT UH

SENIOR & CATALINA.
> THERE CAN BE NO JUSTICE FOR THE DEAD
> THERE CAN BE NO JUSTICE FOR THE DEAD

CATALINA. *(Pointing down the mountain.)* Ooh, yooga dwimmin pooh.

Scene Five

[MUSIC NO. 05A "DRUNKEN TUMACHO"]

*(In the saloon, ***PRUDENCE***, long possessed by Tumacho, sits at a table with a napkin tucked into her dress.)*

*(Manning the kitchen, ***CHAPPY*** *delivers elaborate dishes to* ***PRUDENCE****, then instantly returns to prepare more food.* ***BILL*** *expedites, passing each dish to* ***PRUDENCE*** *with anxious glee, wanting only to please her. Both* ***BILL*** *and* ***CHAPPY*** *wear dirty long johns and boots.)*

*(***CHAPPY*** *brings out a whole fried:)*

CHAPPY. Fish!

BILL. Fish!

PRUDENCE. Fish?!

*(***PRUDENCE*** *picks up the fish and stuffs it down her throat.)*

BILL. Careful, dear. Could be some bones in there –

PRUDENCE. Next.

BILL. Next!

CHAPPY. *(Offstage.)* Already?

BILL. Next!

CHAPPY. *(Offstage.)* Grouse!

*(***CHAPPY*** *emerges with a plate of:)*

BILL. Grouse!

*(Which ***BILL*** *sets before* ***PRUDENCE****, who inhales it.)*

CHAPPY. So, grouse. This is actually a pan-seared grouse. I call it grouse supreme, which means –

BILL. It's a grouse.

PRUDENCE. Yummy.

BILL. A couple of chews, dear, at least one or two?

PRUDENCE. Next!
BILL. Next!
PRUDENCE. Face.
BILL. Face?
PRUDENCE. Face!
BILL. I'm not sure we have any –
PRUDENCE. Gimme your face!
BILL. Yes, dearest.

>   (**BILL** *gives* **PRUDENCE** *his face, which she mauls with licks and kisses.* **CHAPPY** *runs off to the kitchen.*)

PRUDENCE. Thirsty.
BILL. Oh, uh...
PRUDENCE. Thirsty!

>   (**BILL** *hocks up some spit.*)

For beer!
BILL. *(Swallows that.)* Mm, yes. Beer!
CHAPPY. *(Offstage.)* Beer!
PRUDENCE. Beer!
CHAPPY. *(Offstage.)* Coming right up!
PRUDENCE. What's taking so long?
BILL. The chef wants to make sure everything's perfect.
PRUDENCE. *(Flinching in pain.)* Ohh!
BILL. My love? What is it?
PRUDENCE. My tummy. This little corner didn't get a thing. Can you hear him? He says, "What about me?"
BILL. *(Not really.)* Uh-huh?
PRUDENCE. Next!
BILL. Next!

>   (**CHAPPY** *returns, presenting:*)

CHAPPY. Today I've prepared for you a wild boar with tomatillo, which we've paired with a nice hibiscus lager.
PRUDENCE. Boar! Beer! Boar! Beer! Boar! Beer!

BILL. Darling, I hate to interrupt breakfast. But I wonder, perhaps you and I could ride out to the hot springs this weekend –

(**CHAPPY** *exits.*)

PRUDENCE. Could I get some more beer, for crying out loud?

BILL. Doesn't that sound delightful? You and me taking some time away?

PRUDENCE. No. Next!

BILL. But why in heavens not?

PRUDENCE. What if something happens here?

BILL. Like what?

(**CHAPPY** *arrives with a new platter.*)

CHAPPY. Snake bites.

PRUDENCE. What if somebody hosts a party and I'm not here to attend it? I go to parties.

BILL. Yes but –

PRUDENCE. I go to parties!!

CHAPPY. Now I know what you're thinking, but they aren't real snake bites. This is a sausage wrapped in dough, with cheese and olives on top, then I shape it into this fun snake design –

(**PRUDENCE** *grabs hold of* **CHAPPY**'s *butt.*)

PRUDENCE. What's this?

CHAPPY. Oh, Christmas!

PRUDENCE. What do you call this little dish here?

CHAPPY. That would be my derrière.

(**PRUDENCE** *bites* **CHAPPY**'s *butt.*)

PRUDENCE. Snake bite!

(**PRUDENCE** *smacks* **CHAPPY**'s *behind and sends him running back to the kitchen.*)

BILL. What if we just went away for the afternoon?

PRUDENCE. Not in a million years.

BILL. Damn it, darling, I need some time alone with you.

PRUDENCE. *You* need? *You* need?!

[MUSIC NO. 06 "I AM TUMACHO"]

I AM TUMACHO
I AM THE ONE
THE ANGEL WITH A KNIFE IN HIS HEART AND LUST IN
    HIS GUN
I AM TUMACHO
SO YOU'D BETTER SEE
MY SATISFACTION'S THE ONLY THING YOU'LL EVER NEED

BILL. Yes, dear. Anything you say, dear!

PRUDENCE. Next!

BILL. Next!

(Enter **MAYOR EVANS**, *his hair brushed.)*

MAYOR EVANS. Tumacho, I cannot stand idly by while you slurp the goodness out of my people. If they're gonna be your victims in perpetuity, I demand you treat me the same.

PRUDENCE. Next!

*(***BILL** *grabs hold of the* **MAYOR** *and throws him out of the bar.)*

MAYOR EVANS. But –

*(***CHAPPY** *returns with a new platter, which* **PRUDENCE** *devours.)*

CHAPPY. Here we have a candied summer squash.

PRUDENCE. Next!

CHAPPY. But all I got left is a pork roast, and that won't be done for an hour –

PRUDENCE. Next!

BILL. Next!

*(***CHAPPY** *runs back to the kitchen, we hear pots and pans banging, a garbage disposal, a forklift...)*

(The **MAYOR** *re-enters.)*

MAYOR EVANS. Just to reiterate, I'm not asking for anything special. I just want you to do to me what you're doing to everybody else –

PRUDENCE. Next!

MAYOR EVANS. Why won't you punish me?

PRUDENCE. Next!

> (**BILL** *tosses the* **MAYOR** *out of the bar and blocks the door.*)
>
> (**CHAPPY** *returns from the kitchen with:*)

CHAPPY. Pork roast tartare, more or less.

> (**PRUDENCE** *downs it.*)

PRUDENCE. Next!

BILL. I'm afraid that's all the food we have left in town, dear.

PRUDENCE. Did the summer squash count as dessert?

CHAPPY. It always did when I made it for Catalina.

PRUDENCE. Catalina?!

BILL. Catalina?

MAYOR EVANS. *(Popping up in the window.)* Catalina?

PRUDENCE. I never even got a taste! Bring her to me!

> (**BILL** *shuts the window on the* **MAYOR**.)

BILL. But Catalina is gone, dear.

PRUDENCE. Where?!

CHAPPY. To the mountains, to throw herself on the mercy of the gunman Clement Graham.

PRUDENCE. This is an outrage. No Catalina? Bring me the others.

> (**MAYOR EVANS** *appears outside the saloon.*)

MAYOR EVANS. *(Aside.)* I don't appreciate being spurred to action, but that demon gives me no choice. I will bring Catalina back to town, and if Tumacho wants her, he's just gonna have to make a deal.

> (**MAYOR EVANS** *exits.*)

PRUDENCE. Bring me the others!

BILL. Everyone, my love?

PRUDENCE. All at once! This one at a time, this picky-picky, nibble-nibble, it just won't do.

BILL. But dearest, what are your intentions?

PRUDENCE. My intentions are to fill this ancient, rotting void! What are your intentions, William?

BILL. To make you happy. But I cannot do as you have asked.

PRUDENCE. You defy me?

BILL. I know that you think you need their affection, but you don't, because you have mine.

PRUDENCE. I don't care about your affection.

BILL. But I care enough for both of us.

PRUDENCE. Ha! You're gonna gather those buzzards together and you're gonna get 'em all riled up for me, and we're gonna explore the idea of teamwork until I am satisfied.

BILL. Yes, dear. I will do as you say. I will gather them all, and we will give you the night of your life.

PRUDENCE.
> I AM TUMACHO, YES I AM THE ONE
> THE DUDE WITH A RAZOR FOR EYES AND A WHIP FOR A TONGUE
> I AM TUMACHO, AND I KNOW YOU'LL AGREE
> I'M GONNA GET SOME FROM EVERY LAST ONE
> THEY WERE RIGHT, IT IS FUN WHEN YOU'RE BIG AS THE SUN
> I AM TUMACHO
> THE BEAST LIVES IN ME!

Scene Six

(Wobbly traveling music.*)

(A tiny puppet Mayor Evans rides fast on a tiny horse up a tiny mountain. He encounters a tiny vendor on a tiny mule.)

MAYOR EVANS. *(Offstage. Exhausted.)* Oof, hello there. Large watermelon juice. And some of those spicy cucumbers.

(Drinks his juice.)

Ahh. Thank you. I like your cape.

(The tiny mayor races on.)

(Then...)

(Groovy, grand hacienda guitar.*)

(The hacienda belonging to Clement Graham Sr. **CATALINA** *is now dressed exceedingly well. A full-sized* **MAYOR EVANS** *has just arrived after the long journey.* **CATALINA** *reads a letter – it is not super well-written.)*

CATALINA. "Dear Ms. Vucovich–Villalobos, we are please to announce you as one of ten lucky winners in the Free Lotto draw held yesterday."

MAYOR EVANS. Yeah, that would've been a few days ago now.

CATALINA. Uh-huh. "Your name emerged alongside nine others, and consequently, you have been approved for a total payout of 250,000 gold coin dollars."

MAYOR EVANS. 250,000? Do you have any idea how much money that is?

---

*Samuel French licenses optional incidental music by Ian M. Riggs. If you choose not to license this optional music, please be aware that a license to produce *Tumacho* does not include a performance license for any third-party or copyrighted music. Licensees should create an original composition or use music in the public domain. For further information, please see the Music and Third-Party Materials Use Note on page iii.

CATALINA. "The following particulars are attached to your lotto payment. You must come home to the town you love dearly."

MAYOR EVANS. Anything else? What about the fine print?

CATALINA. "That is it. That is all you must do. Simply come home, to where life has returned to once again being really good. Then you will get to keep all these gold coin dollars."

MAYOR EVANS. Heck, Catalina, congratulations!

CATALINA. *(Not buying it.)* Thanks.

MAYOR EVANS. I didn't know what the fuss was about. "Good news," that's all they told me.

CATALINA. Who's they?

MAYOR EVANS. The people who administrate the prize.

CATALINA. And who would that be?

MAYOR EVANS. Anonymous donors, friends of friends.

CATALINA. And life back home has "returned to once again being really good," huh?

MAYOR EVANS. That's what it says.

CATALINA. I'm asking your opinion.

MAYOR EVANS. Yup. Things have never been sweeter.

CATALINA. I'm glad to hear it. But I don't need the money.

MAYOR EVANS. Come on, everybody needs –

(Spotting a great structure.)

Is that an amphitheater?

CATALINA. A pavilion.

MAYOR EVANS. Well, you do seem nicely situated here. But 250,000 dollars! No one can say no to that.

CATALINA. Give it to Alice.

MAYOR EVANS. Alice?

CATALINA. She could use it, couldn't she?

MAYOR EVANS. *(Stifling an urge to cry.)* Oh, Alice could use a lot of things. But, well okay then, if you'll just come on home, I'll make sure the funds get transferred.

CATALINA. I'm not eligible to receive this prize, Mayor Evans.

MAYOR EVANS. But of course you are!

CATALINA. "Must come home to the town you love dearly." See that?

MAYOR EVANS. Yeah?

CATALINA. Well, I don't have an ounce of love for that place, and I never will again. I think it's best if you go on back now.

MAYOR EVANS. *(Defeated.)* Okay.

(He sneakily tries to take her hand and bring her with, but she slips his grip.)

CATALINA. Goodbye, Mayor Evans.

MAYOR EVANS. *(Dropping to his knees.)* Please. Hate me, besmirch me, throw dirt in my face, but come home. They need you.

CATALINA. I thought you said everything was going so well.

MAYOR EVANS. No. The truth is, Tumacho has returned –

CATALINA. Uh–huh –

MAYOR EVANS. – In the form of Prudence Alderman –

CATALINA. How many lies can you fit into one rotten mouth?

MAYOR EVANS. And he turned Bill into his slave. Chappy too, Doc, Sam, even Alice, everyone except for me.

CATALINA. And why has the demon spared you?

MAYOR EVANS. I don't know! I kept throwing myself at him, but he wouldn't have me! And it felt awful. I mean, it's one thing having to suffer with other people, but having to watch while they suffer without you? That's just too much.

CATALINA. What do you expect me to do about it?

MAYOR EVANS. Well, Tumacho did express an interest in your company.

CATALINA. He did, did he?

MAYOR EVANS. Yeah.

CATALINA. Well, why didn't you just come out and say that? Why do you always have to try to trick people with some phony promise?

MAYOR EVANS. It's the skill I have. Plus in this case I was thinking of trading you for everyone else, which would've been hard to explain. Maybe you have other ideas? Catalina, they're in trouble.

CATALINA. *(After a moment of reflection.)* Okay, I've been doing a lot of work on myself?

MAYOR EVANS. Uh-huh?

CATALINA. And a big moment for me was when I realized that if I can't have revenge, and I can't have forgiveness or live in a town where the grown-ups act like grown-ups, then at least I can have soft pillows. Nice clothes. Good food and someone kind to share my life with. Do you see what I'm getting at?

MAYOR EVANS. It sounds like you're recommending personal comfort as a salve against worldly injustice.

CATALINA. For me. I'm just saying, that's what works for me.

MAYOR EVANS. Would you be open to me coming to live with you guys?

CATALINA. No, that is your town. Those are your people. They've got a problem and you need to fix it.

MAYOR EVANS. But I can't do it alone.

CATALINA. You don't have a choice.

MAYOR EVANS. You're right.

(Standing, dusting himself off.)

I'll say this, though, Catalina. You are eligible to win that prize.

CATALINA. There is no prize.

MAYOR EVANS. I concede that –

CATALINA. There are no gold coin dollars –

MAYOR EVANS. I'm just saying, if there was a prize! You would be eligible. And I think you know it.

*(**MAYOR EVANS** starts to go.)*

CATALINA. You see that fella down there with the wheelbarrow, picking cabbage with his shirt off?

MAYOR EVANS. *(Looks.)* The glisteny one?
CATALINA. That's what I call a prize.
MAYOR EVANS. He's been good to you, has he?
CATALINA. The best.
(Against her better judgment.) Come on.

> *(In an instant, the* **MAYOR** *calls for their horses, and* **CATALINA** *and* **MAYOR EVANS** *are riding down the mountain.)*

[MUSIC NO. 07 "HERE I GO"]

HERE I GO, I'M ON MY WAY
I'M COMIN' HOME FOR JUDGMENT DAY

MAYOR EVANS & CATALINA.
I'M ON MY WAY, I'M ON MY WAY

MAYOR EVANS.
TELL MY FAM'LY AND MY FRIENDS
I WILL TRY TO MAKE AMENDS

MAYOR EVANS & CATALINA.
I'M ON MY WAY, I'M ON MY WAY
AND I WILL LEARN...

MAYOR EVANS.
I WILL LEARN TO LOVE MY BURDENS

MAYOR EVANS & CATALINA.
AND I WILL LEAVE...

CATALINA.
I WILL LEAVE BEHIND REGRET

MAYOR EVANS & CATALINA.
AND ALL THE DUMB...

MAYOR EVANS.
ALL THE DUMB THINGS I ASSERTED

MAYOR EVANS & CATALINA.
LET THE LORD FORGIVE IF NOT FORGET

CATALINA.
AND IF THEY FIND A PLACE FOR ME
TO REST MY HEAD ETERNALLY

MAYOR EVANS & CATALINA.
MY HEART WILL SING, MY HEART WILL SING,
I'M COMING HOME – HOME, HOME, HOME, HOME
I'M COMING HOME – HOME, HOME, HOME, HOME

(The tempo quickens.)

I'M COMING HOME – HOME, HOME, HOME, HOME
HOME, HOME, HOME, HOME

*(**MAYOR EVANS** and **CATALINA** are attacked by a jaguar, but **CATALINA** fights it off.)*

AND IF THEY FIND A PLACE FOR ME
TO REST MY HEAD ETERNALLY
MY HEART WILL SING, MY HEART WILL SING

*(They are joined in song by **CACTI**.)*

MAYOR EVANS, CATALINA & CACTI.
I'M COMING HOME – HOME, HOME, HOME, HOME
I'M COMING HOME – HOME, HOME, HOME, HOME
I'M COMING HOME – HOME, HOME, HOME, HOME
HOME, HOME, HOME, HOME

Scene Seven

(In the saloon, **DR. ALONZO, SAM, ALICE, CHAPPY,** *and* **BILL** *have gathered, all clad in dirty long johns that now seem a few sizes too big for them – suggesting perhaps that they're all wasting away.)*

BILL. Now Sam, you lean back on the bar. Just a bit more. And tip your hat up. Yeah, like you been out in the field all day and aim to catch a breeze. But keep your eyes open, if you can. That's it. Oh, you're a bad man now, Sam. You're gonna need an extra-special ravaging.

SAM. Yeah I am.

BILL. Okay, Chappy, go back to where you were on the other side of the bar, but scrunch down. Yeah, like you're working on something. Oh, you're cooking up something good now, ain't ya? Whatcha got cooking, Chappy?

CHAPPY. I'm making hamburgers.

DR. ALONZO. He means like a plan.

CHAPPY. Oh.

BILL. Whatcha planning, Chappy Wing?

CHAPPY. Night raid.

BILL. Look out, everybody. Chappy Wing is on a night raid.

CHAPPY. Caw, caw...

BILL. Alice, could I just see your sleeves up? Nice. And sleeves down? And hide your hands inside the sleeves? And elbows out? Show me the teapot? Good.

(To **DR. ALONZO.***)* Now, Doctor Alonzo, I like this. There ain't a thing wrong with what we have here. But is there anything you could do that might be just a bit dirtier?

DR. ALONZO. Like what?

BILL. I'm just thinking if everyone else is kinda genteel and come-hither, but if you're sorta like an extra-extra-dirty rascal, something like that?

> (**DR. ALONZO** *attempts to make a dirty gesture [which in fact is totally un-dirty, like flapping arms or something 100% nonsensical].*)

BILL. And if it was something not so chickeny?

> (**DR. ALONZO** *tones down the gesture.*)
>
> (**SAM** *now tries his own dirty thing. [All the dirty things should be strange and abstract; not at all dirty.]*)

SAM. Like this?

ALICE. *(Trying something.)* Or this?

BILL. No.

CHAPPY. *(Trying something.)* I can do this.

ALICE. *(Trying what* **CHAPPY** *tried.)* We can do it together.

BILL. No, no, everybody stop! Only Doctor Alonzo, the rest…go back to your positions!

> (*Everyone goes back to their previous pose, except* **DR. ALONZO**, *who keeps doing his dirty thing.*)

Okay, Doctor, that's fine. Just…cut it out! Reset!

> (**DR. ALONZO** *stops his dirty thing. All return to their original positions.*)

Now all of you, stay as you are. Don't move anywhere or do anything. One last time, let's review: what is our goal tonight?

ALL. To satisfy our master.

BILL. And how do we do that?

ALL. By giving him what he wants.

BILL. That's right. Now remember, no showmanship. No bonus kisses or extra time – he don't like it and he don't need it. Just stick to your assignments. Let yourself be ravaged in the fashion we discussed, then step aside. Sam, you'll go first, and I'll go last.

(To himself.) And spend eternity in the warm embrace of his immortal soul.

    (**BILL** *exits. It's quiet.*)

ALICE. Still think we're better off?

DR. ALONZO. I never said we're better off –

ALICE.	**SAM.**	**CHAPPY.**
Yeah you did.	Sure you did.	That's exactly what you said.

DR. ALONZO. I said on an emotional level, it wasn't so bad having a break from Bill's reign of terror.

ALICE.	**SAM.**	**CHAPPY.**
I don't know.	I don't think so.	I think the words were different.

DR. ALONZO. And many of you agreed, if I recall correctly.

ALICE.	**SAM.**	**CHAPPY.**
Well.	At first.	It had been a difficult winter.

DR. ALONZO. I certainly never imagined that we would be getting ravaged every day.

ALICE.	**SAM.**	**CHAPPY.**
No.	Me neither.	Maybe every other day.

DR. ALONZO. And I'm not going to say that Tumacho is the all-time worst ravager ever.

ALICE.	**SAM.**	**CHAPPY.**
No.	A lot of finesse actually	Did he do the cartwheel thing with you?
Backwards.	Sage brush.	Apple sauce.

DR. ALONZO. But the darkness, when it comes…

ALICE, SAM & CHAPPY. The darkness.

DR. ALONZO. It's just so very dark. And am I wrong or is it getting darker?

ALICE.	**SAM.**	**CHAPPY.**
No, it's getting darker.	Much darker.	When I close my eyes it all goes black.

ALICE. *(A confession, even to herself.)* I don't want to be ravaged anymore.

SAM. Me neither.

DR. ALONZO. I thought I was the only one.

CHAPPY. No.

ALICE. I mean, I've always been a go-with-the-flow type of person. You know, if it feels bad, it's probably 'cause it should. But at some point you have to ask: is this any way to live?

DR. ALONZO, SAM & CHAPPY. No!

DR. ALONZO. How low had our expectations sunk?

ALICE.	**SAM.**	**CHAPPY.**
Real low.	Bottom of the barrel.	They were like centipedes.

DR. ALONZO. How bad had our lives become that we somehow deemed this current situation to be tolerable?

ALICE, SAM & CHAPPY. Bad!

DR. ALONZO. We've been like a bunch of vultures: starving, desperate; willing to take whatever scraps the wicked world throws our way. But damn it, I want something better.

ALICE.	**SAM.**	**CHAPPY.**
Yeah.	Yeah.	Me too.

ALICE. Let's kill us a demon!

DR. ALONZO, SAM & CHAPPY. Yeah!

DR. ALONZO. But how? We know bullets won't hurt him.

ALICE. There's more than one way to skin a cat, Doc.

CHAPPY. That's true, you can do a zip cut or you can braise it first.

ALICE. What if we dropped a church bell on top of his head?

DR. ALONZO. Not bad. Only trouble is, he doesn't go to church.

CHAPPY. What if I made him a birthday cake with dynamite inside?

DR. ALONZO. That's a nice offer, Chappy, but his birthday isn't 'til February.

ALICE. We could run him over with horses.

DR. ALONZO, SAM & CHAPPY. *(That's a cool idea.)* Ooooh…

DR. ALONZO. I like that.

ALICE. Would it work?

DR. ALONZO. I can't say, but it's the best plan I've heard so far.

CHAPPY. I still like the birthday cake first, and then the horse.

ALICE. The church bell is my favorite, then the horse and then the birthday cake, but it might depend on who's riding the horse.

SAM. "When the scoundrel's heart is vanquished and the dragon sings his song, the butterfly will flap her wings until Tumacho's gone."

DR. ALONZO. *(Ignoring that.)* Or we could drown him in sewage.

> *(The **MAYOR** and **CATALINA** appear outside the bar.)*

CATALINA. *(As if having an asthma attack.)* Wait, I can't go in there.

MAYOR EVANS. Why?

CATALINA. They're having a meeting.

MAYOR EVANS. So?

CATALINA. I can't work in groups.

MAYOR EVANS. Sure you can –

CATALINA. No, no, I already want to punch somebody –

MAYOR EVANS. Catalina –

CATALINA. Don't…like…people…must…have…whiskey!

MAYOR EVANS. Look at me! If things get heated, you just remind yourself – this is a little trick I learned long ago – only listen to the things you want to hear.

CATALINA. *(Considers.)* Okay, let's go.

    *(**CATALINA** and the **MAYOR** enter the bar.)*

MAYOR EVANS. Guten abend!

DR. ALONZO. You're back!

MAYOR EVANS. Another slumber party without me, eh, Doc?

ALICE. Catalina, I thought you got away for good.

CATALINA. Yeah, well, so did I.

CHAPPY. Catalina!

    *(**CHAPPY** gives her a big hug, then pushes her away, heading out.)*

If you'll excuse me, I have another obligation.

CATALINA. Chappy, I'm sorry. I'm sorry I left.

CHAPPY. Do you have any idea what we've been through? We have been getting ravaged by a demon!

ALICE. Chappy, be nice.

CHAPPY. I'm frustrated!

    (A breath.)

I thought you was dead.

CATALINA. I understand you being upset. I really do. I just needed to change some things, and I didn't have the courage you all had, to try to do that here.

ALICE. But we haven't really changed anything.

CATALINA. Maybe we could do that now?

DR. ALONZO.	**SAM.**	**CHAPPY.**	**ALICE.**
Maybe.	Possible.	I guess.	Suppose so.

CATALINA. Anybody here wanna kill us a demon?

DR. ALONZO, SAM, CHAPPY & ALICE. Yeah!

CATALINA. Okay, here's what we're gonna do. Mayor Evans?

MAYOR EVANS. It's pretty interesting, as Catalina and I were headed back to town, we didn't have any preconceived notions about how to deal with Tumacho specifically. Rather, we decided to look for a larger idea, a more long-term solution to dealing with bullies and brutes of all kinds. And what we arrived at was –

CATALINA. We're gonna run 'em over with horses!

DR. ALONZO, SAM, CHAPPY & ALICE. Awww, bawww, come on –

CATALINA. What?!

CHAPPY. We already came up with horses!

CATALINA. How?

CHAPPY. How?! What do you mean how?

ALICE. You're not the only ones capable of coming up with a plan.

DR. ALONZO. Settle down! Everyone, please. Unless I'm mistaken, we are all in agreement – for the first time ever. Now, do the technical aspects still have to be coordinated? Yes. But is the mission clear? I think it is.

ALICE. Wait. Has anyone considered what lies beneath the demon's gnarly shell?

CHAPPY. I have, I think it's nougat.

CATALINA. Prudence.

ALICE. If we run over Tumacho with horses, what'll become of her?

SAM. "When the scoundrel's heart is vanquished and the dragon sings his song, the butterfly will flap her wings until Tumacho's gone."

MAYOR EVANS. *(Ignoring that.)* What if, when we trample Tumacho, we do it over a bed of pine needles, so Prudence only gets half-squished?

CATALINA. Wait, Sam, what did you just say?

SAM. Oh, I don't know. Maybe it was something like, "Ignore the elderly at your peril."

ALICE. Grandpa, say it again.

SAM. "When the scoundrel's heart is vanquished and the dragon sings his song, the butterfly will flap her wings until Tumacho's gone."

DR. ALONZO. The scoundrel's heart, that's Bill.

CATALINA. How do you mean?

DR. ALONZO. He's head over heels for Tumacho. If the demon said even an unkind word, Yardley would crumble to pieces.

CHAPPY. The butterfly is you, Catalina.

CATALINA. Chappy, I'm trying to – no, you know what? A Catalina is a kind of butterfly.

DR. ALONZO. So you'll have to do most of the talking.

CATALINA. Right.

MAYOR EVANS. Now if only we had a dragon who could sing a fiery song.

ALICE. Ignatius. It's you.

MAYOR EVANS. Why would you say that?

ALICE. Uh, I don't want to...

SAM. It's your breath.

MAYOR EVANS. What about it?

DR. ALONZO. Evans, you have a certain fragrance.

MAYOR EVANS. Are you saying...you all have independently concluded that I have an issue in this department?

CHAPPY. Yes.

ALICE. It's not so bad.

CATALINA. We all got used to it long ago.

SAM. Mayor, your breath is like demon poison.

MAYOR EVANS. Well Sam, your face is like a porcupine's asshole.

DR. ALONZO, SAM, CHAPPY, ALICE & CATALINA. Hey, now –

MAYOR EVANS. I'm sick of people talking bad about me!

SAM. I'm just saying, that must be why Tumacho never ravaged you, because your breath is like a repellent to him.

MAYOR EVANS. *(Considers; backing off.)* I guess I wasn't hearing it that way.

CATALINA. It's not your fault, Mayor Evans.

MAYOR EVANS. No. But it is my responsibility. I will make the demon taste my kiss.

ALICE. Won't that be dangerous?

DR. ALONZO. Alice, I don't think we have another choice.

MAYOR EVANS. I'm afraid the doctor is right.

SAM. But the demon won't even get near him.

CATALINA. Mayor, give me your coat.

> *(The **MAYOR** gives her his coat –)*

Better give me the mustache too.

> *(– And his mustache.)*
>
> *(A noise is heard from down the street.)*

CHAPPY. They're coming!

CATALINA. Chappy and Sam, you make sure Yardley's heart gets vanquished, and then we're gonna...

> *(**CATALINA** whispers the rest of the plan as the **OTHERS** crowd in to listen.)*

One-two-three!

ALL. Big plays all day!

> *(**ALICE**, **DR. ALONZO**, and the **MAYOR** follow **CATALINA** into the bathroom.)*
>
> *(**BILL** enters, plucking a banjo, followed by **PRUDENCE**, who dances like Salome – until she sees the others are gone.)*

PRUDENCE. What is the meaning of this?

BILL. Where have they gone? They were given clear instructions –

PRUDENCE. I warned you.

CHAPPY. Catalina's back.

BILL. Catalina?!

PRUDENCE. Catalina?! At last!

SAM. Mayor Evans has her tied up for you in the town square.

PRUDENCE. Who needs vermin when I can have steak?

BILL. Darling, give me another chance. I will gather them up for you and I will –

PRUDENCE. You are dead to me. And you will never know my ravaging again.

> (**PRUDENCE** *exits.*)
>
> (**BILL** *starts after her, but* **CHAPPY** *and* **SAM** *block his way.* **BILL** *collapses in despair.*)

Scene Eight

(In the town square, **DR. ALONZO** *dresses up* **MAYOR EVANS** *to look like Catalina, then ties him to a tree.)*

[MUSIC NO. 08 "ALICE'S WORRIES (AM I TUMACHO? - REPRISE)"]

(Meanwhile, as if providing cover, an anxious **ALICE** *sings a Spanish bird version of "Am I Tumacho?," replacing all the words with "la.")*

(Once the **MAYOR** *is tied up,* **ALICE** *and* **DR. ALONZO** *exit.)*

*(***PRUDENCE** *backs her way into the square, keeping an eye on* **CATALINA***, who she believes to be the mayor, because she is dressed like him.)*

CATALINA. *(Re: the* **MAYOR***.)* Here she is.

*(***PRUDENCE** *turns to see the* **MAYOR** *– as Catalina – tied to the tree.)*

PRUDENCE. Oh, where did you find her?

CATALINA. Well, I was riding up Sandhill Pass, when through a bramble I spotted her drinking from a crick.

PRUDENCE. Like a little fawn.

CATALINA. Yes.

PRUDENCE. How thrilling.

CATALINA. Of course, it wasn't easy taking her into custody –

PRUDENCE. No.

CATALINA. Governance is more my especiality. But I knew she was worthy of your attention, so I did what I had to do.

PRUDENCE. Very kind of you to scoop her up.

(As **PRUDENCE** *approaches, the* **MAYOR** *takes an enormous breath and holds it.)*

PRUDENCE. You've done yourself proud, Evans. Who'd have thought, after all these years, you could actually get something done?

CATALINA. Well, if you knew me as the other people in this town do –

PRUDENCE. They complain about you constantly. I can't think – wait, can I? No, I can't think of anyone with a less impressive reputation.

CATALINA. I have long been preparing for the moment when I could do my part.

PRUDENCE. If you say so.

CATALINA. And I have always understood that complaining is just their way of saying "we care." No matter how dissatisfied they may seem, I know I can rely on the people of this town.

PRUDENCE. I used to think I could rely on people.

CATALINA. Must be hard to keep friends when you're a crazy demon.

PRUDENCE. What'd you say?!

CATALINA. Nothing.

PRUDENCE. His name was Richard Curly. He ran a gang that took over our town, and he stole whatever he wanted: chickens, money, people. One day he kidnapped my beloved Mathilde. I went to my neighbors and begged them to help me rescue her, but they all turned their backs to me – the cobbler, the butcher, the priest; buried their faces in beer and said there was nothing to be done. So one afternoon I broke into Curly's compound. I snuck past the guards and found Mathilde in the kitchen, making corn soup. She was a wonderful cook. I told her to follow me out, but Mathilde said no. She said she had fallen in love with Curly, and that soon they'd be moving away together. To Montreal. Which is in Canada. "Don't ever think of me again," she said. I went home and tried to do as she'd asked, but I thought of her every second. So I went back to Curly's and set fire to the compound, and then I watched it burn with Mathilde inside. Curly escaped. He rode off into the desert, and when I finally caught up to him, he told me he'd been there that day, listening from the other room. Mathilde knew he would kill me if she tried to go with me, so she lied to my face to spare me. "Her love was yours," said Curly, "until you burned her alive." I ripped the heart out of his chest. Then I rode back to town and ravaged them all, the cobbler, the priest, everyone who refused to help me and everybody they knew. Which is what I do each time I return. I feast and hope the void will be filled. Hungry. Always hungry. But not crazy.

CATALINA. Catalina once sought revenge when the town failed to help her, and in that situation as well, an innocent person was killed.

PRUDENCE. Yes, Mayor Evans. I know.

> (**PRUDENCE** *goes in to kiss* **MAYOR EVANS** *but backs off, gagging.*)

Oof. Little bit of nausea there. Probably didn't get enough sleep. Okay.

> (**PRUDENCE** *puckers up to the* **MAYOR** *again as* **BILL** *runs into the square, followed by everyone else.*)

BILL. Tumacho, my dearest, don't do it!

PRUDENCE. What, this?

> (**PRUDENCE** *goes to* **MAYOR EVANS**, *kissing him deeply. Time stops. The two are overcome with kiss.*)
>
> (*Soon,* **PRUDENCE**'s *eyes widen as if she had eaten a bucket of peppers. Her arms flail, her body squirms, and smoke comes out of her ears until – in a blast – she is flung to the ground.*)
>
> (**BILL** *goes to her limp body and holds her.*)

[MUSIC NO. 09 "DEMON DOLL"]

BILL.
>THE MOON WON'T SHINE WITHOUT THE SUN
>THE SPRING WON'T COME WITHOUT THE FALL
>AND I WON'T EVER BE THE SAME AGAIN
>WITHOUT MY DEMON DOLL
>
>THEY SAID I WAS SO ROTTEN
>I TORE THE WHOLE WIDE WORLD APART
>MY GAINS WERE ALL ILL-GOTTEN
>BUT I NEVER KNEW BAD 'TIL I GAVE YOU MY HEART
>
>A BIRD CAN'T FLY WITHOUT ITS WING
>A BEE WON'T BUZZ IF IT CAN'T STING
>AND I DON'T CARE ABOUT ANYTHING
>WITHOUT MY DEMON DOLL
>WITHOUT MY DOLL

PRUDENCE. *(Opening her eyes.)* Is that –?

>*(Chokes, coughs, gets her bell rung, choo-choos, whinnies, and then, as herself:)*

...Get your hands off me.

DR. ALONZO. Prudence, it's you!

>*(The others cheer.* **DR. ALONZO** *pulls* **BILL** *away from* **PRUDENCE** *as* **ALICE** *goes to* **MAYOR EVANS.***)*

ALICE. Ignatius, you did it. You came through.

>*(***MAYOR EVANS** *smiles, his eyes glazed.)*

Ignatius? Are you okay?

MAYOR EVANS. What a feeling.

>*(A bigger cheer.* **ALICE** *unties the* **MAYOR.***)*

PRUDENCE. Will someone please explain what has happened to me?

CATALINA. Prudence, I'm afraid you have undergone a serious possession.

PRUDENCE. Was I...?

CATALINA. Yes.

PRUDENCE. Did I...?
CATALINA. Yes.
PRUDENCE. To everyone?
CATALINA. *Almost* everyone.
PRUDENCE. Oh my. I didn't "enjoy it," did I?
ALICE & SAM. Eh...
DR. ALONZO. Well...
CHAPPY. Now that you mention it...
CATALINA. *(Trying to protect* **PRUDENCE.***)* No –
ALICE & SAM. No.
DR. ALONZO. Definitely not.
CHAPPY. Not very much.
PRUDENCE. Good! You know, I have always tried to be a model of civility and virtue, to raise the standards for moral and upright living –
CATALINA. Ugh.
ALICE. Please.
SAM. Great.
DR. ALONZO. So happy to see you.
CHAPPY. Welcome back.

>   (**SAM** *sits down by the tree.* **DR. ALONZO** *starts to lead* **BILL** *away.)*

CATALINA. Doc, where are you going?
DR. ALONZO. Oh, I'm just gonna take Bill out behind the bar and shoot him.
PRUDENCE, SAM, CHAPPY, ALICE & CATALINA. Whoa!
CATALINA. Doc, you can't go shooting Bill.
DR. ALONZO. Why not?
CATALINA. Because it isn't right.
DR. ALONZO. Catalina, this tyrant has been wreaking havoc on our lives for years. He's spilled gallons of blood and most of it's ended up on me. I don't sleep. I don't dream. I take drugs, but they don't help. I mean, they help a little but not really. Every time I close my eyes I

see the face of someone who died in my arms because of him. Give me one good reason why he should get to live.

BILL. Because I'm human.

CATALINA. No, Bill. Because we are.

BILL. I'm human too.

CATALINA. I know that, and you have done some terrible things. But so have I, so have we all. And every time one of us tries to settle that score, an innocent person gets hurt and a demon shows up. So this time we're going to do the opposite. We're gonna open our hearts to him.

ALICE.	**MAYOR.**	**PRUDENCE.**	**CHAPPY.**
Eww.	Gross.	That's disgusting.	No way.

DR. ALONZO. I can't open my heart to Bill.

CATALINA. If he can open his heart to Tumacho, we can at least try.

PIRATE. Chirp chirp chirp!

ALICE. Pirate, no!

(*PIRATE enters, and* **BILL** *scoops him up.*)

BILL. Nobody move or I'll break the coyote's neck.

ALICE. Get your hands off my Pirate –

BILL. Or what? Whatcha gonna do, Alice? Catalina, do you think I want to live in a town where bygones are bygones? You think that would be a *good* thing for me? Let me be clear: my intentions are bad; I don't like any of you; and my heart is a million percent closed forever. Also –

CHAPPY. Bill, did I ever tell you how much I enjoyed your mentorship?

BILL. Chappy, please don't interrupt. That does not feel good to me!

CHAPPY. Oh, I'm sorry. I was just thinking how much I respect you, and how sad I am to know that you would like to hurt Pirate. Didn't you once have a dog yourself?

BILL. We don't talk about Ginger.

CHAPPY. Okay. But didn't Ginger run away?

BILL. She was stolen!

CHAPPY. Wow, so, just imagine how Alice would feel if something happened to Pirate. And then consider handing Pirate over to me or really to anybody and replacing that anger with something positive, like – do you have any hobbies?

BILL. No.

CATALINA. What about leather-working?

BILL. I did enjoy leather-working once.

CHAPPY. So why not try giving that another shot?

>   (**BILL** *gives* **PIRATE** *to* **CHAPPY**, *who gives him to* **ALICE**, *and the people cheer.*)

CATALINA. Chappy, that's the best hostage negotiation I've ever seen!

CHAPPY. I knew I could do it! I just had to get out of my own way!

>   (*The people cheer. The* **MAYOR**, *who has been fiddling with his mouth, pulls out a small nugget.*)

MAYOR EVANS. Yes! Thank you, Lord! Oh my god! Hell yeah! Yes!

CATALINA. What's that?

MAYOR EVANS. It's a peppercorn from a piece of salami I stole from my neighbor Stuart when I was ten.

OTHERS. Ew...

MAYOR EVANS. I never thought I'd get it, but the demon musta lodged it free. Woo, does that feel good!

DR. ALONZO. Speaking of vittles, I got a stash of half-priced potatoes from Laredo back at my place!

CATALINA. Who's hungry?

>   (*More cheers. They start to head off.*)

ALICE. Come on, Grandpa. Grandpa?

> *(**SAM** isn't moving. His eyes are shut. **ALICE** goes to him as the others hold.)*

ALICE. Is he...gone?

DR. ALONZO. *(Checking on **SAM**.)* It appears to be...natural causes.

MAYOR EVANS. I can't remember the last time you said that.

> *(They all take a moment to reflect. Somber church piano.* **BILL** goes to pick up **SAM** in his arms, and the other **MEN** help carry him off.)*

---

*Samuel French licenses optional incidental music by Ian M. Riggs. If you choose not to license this optional music, please be aware that a license to produce *Tumacho* does not include a performance license for any third-party or copyrighted music. Licensees should create an original composition or use music in the public domain. For further information, please see the Music and Third-Party Materials Use Note on page iii.

EPILOGUE

(Modern, hopeful country guitar, somehow evoking the Ramones.*)

(The town square. A parade unfolds. Each time a float goes by, it features just about everyone who lives here dressed as a shrub or animal. **CATALINA** *and* **MAYOR EVANS** *take in the scene.* **CATALINA** *wears a star.)*

MAYOR EVANS. Sheriff, you have really exceeded all expectations.

CATALINA. Well, Mayor Evans, we figured you deserve it.

MAYOR EVANS. I don't know about that.

CATALINA. Come on. We wouldn't be here without you.

MAYOR EVANS. But to have a whole parade in my honor, and then have you rename the town after me?

CATALINA. Yeah, we're not renaming the town after you.

MAYOR EVANS. Well, you know, to put it on the ballot as a measure?

CATALINA. That's not happening.

MAYOR EVANS. For this one street? Evans Boulevard? I love it. It's just wonderful. The whole day.

(Fighting off tears.)

Really just a wonderful day.

---

*Samuel French licenses optional incidental music by Ian M. Riggs. If you choose not to license this optional music, please be aware that a license to produce *Tumacho* does not include a performance license for any third-party or copyrighted music. Licensees should create an original composition or use music in the public domain. For further information, please see the Music and Third-Party Materials Use Note on page iii.

CATALINA. What's wrong?

MAYOR EVANS. I don't know. Maybe it's Alice.

CATALINA. Well, she always wanted to move away.

MAYOR EVANS. I know.

CATALINA. I think it's gonna be good for her. Especially now that Sam's passed on. It's her time to build a life.

MAYOR EVANS. Yeah. It's just hard, you know, 'cause of how close we were.

CATALINA. I didn't know.

MAYOR EVANS. It was pretty intense. She couldn't talk about it really, or think about it.

CATALINA. Well, maybe that's the kind of special connection that'll stay strong even from a distance.

MAYOR EVANS. You think that sorta thing ever works out?

CATALINA. Do I?

(CATALINA whistles, and CLEMENT GRAHAM SR. enters, wearing a smaller star.)

SENIOR. Hey there, we're ready for ya.

CATALINA. Well, you don't give the orders around here, deputy.

SENIOR. Yeah, yeah, yeah –

CATALINA. *(To the MAYOR.)* I like showing him who's in charge.

(To SENIOR.) Re-organize my desk!

SENIOR. Come on now, boss, you're almost up.

(SENIOR exits.)

CATALINA. *(About to leave, then.)* Mayor, you're not planning on leaving town yourself, are you?

MAYOR EVANS. Me? No.

CATALINA. Good. 'Cause we got a meeting on Monday, and that agenda is long.

MAYOR EVANS. Don't I know it.

CATALINA. Well, here's Alice. I'll let you two say goodbye.

*(**CATALINA** exits. Soon after, she and **SENIOR** join the next float.)*

*(**MAYOR EVANS** waves to **ALICE**, who remains offstage.)*

MAYOR EVANS. Hi there.

ALICE. *(Offstage.)* Goodbye!

MAYOR EVANS. Oh, okay, I guess that's it then. Have fun. I'll send you letters...if you send me letters...
(After a moment, to himself.) Hm. Cool.

(Watching the parade a moment, making himself be present.)

Oh, look at this parade. Prairie dogs! What a beautiful town.

*(**ALICE** runs on and gives the **MAYOR** a piece of paper and a schoolgirl hug.)*

ALICE. Write to me.

MAYOR EVANS. Yes.

*(**ALICE** runs off. He reads the paper.)*

45378774 Mulberry Street. Oh, Alice. That's...that's too many numbers.

*(A float enters with the townsfolk – including **CLEMENT** and **CATALINA** – posing as shrubs and animals. Atop the float, **CHAPPY** is dressed as a cactus.)*

[MUSIC NO. 10 "OH, THE SAGUARO"]

ALL BUT MAYOR EVANS.
OH THE SAGUARO
OH THE SAGUARO
OH THE SAGUARO...HM

OH THE SAGUARO
HE LOOKS SO PRICKLY,
LIKE HE DON'T LIKE YOUR FACE
BUT HIS FRUIT IS SO
TENDER AND JUICY

ALL BUT MAYOR EVANS.
>JUST WAIT UNTIL YOU TASTE
>YES IT TAKES PRACTICE
>TO LOVE A CACTUS
>
>OH THE SAGUARO
>OH THE SAGUARO
>OH THE SAGUARO...HM

>*(**BILL** enters, holding a belt, and comes up behind **MAYOR EVANS**.)*

BILL. Mayor Evans?

MAYOR EVANS. *(Cowering.)* Bill?

BILL. I made this for you. For your pants.

>*(The **MAYOR** puts on the belt and pulls up his pants.)*

Keep 'em up there.

MAYOR EVANS. I'll try. Now you stay right here.

>*(The **MAYOR** exits, then joins the float. All of the townspeople sing to **BILL**.)*

CHAPPY.
>YES IT TAKES PRACTICE
>TO LOVE A CACTUS

ALL BUT BILL.
>OH THE SAGUARO
>OH THE SAGUARO
>OH THE SAGUARO...HM

End of Play

www.ingramcontent.com/pod-product-compliance
Lightning Source LLC
Chambersburg PA
CBHW051410290426
44108CB00015B/2233